Orchids

Andrew Mikolajski

Orchids

Photography : Deirdre Rooney

MARABOUT

what is an orchid?

With their flamboyant, intriguing flowers, orchids have long fascinated gardeners and non-gardeners alike. Once the preserve of wealthy connoisseurs, they enjoyed a vogue in the 1960s as glamorous corsages for debs and duchesses. After a brief eclipse, they are newly popular as never before. And rightly so. Extensive breeding has produced a vast range of plants that seem to produce an endless succession of beautiful flowers. And they are no longer the hothouse divas of yesteryear. A significant majority are accommodating, easy-to-care-for plants that will perform reliably over a long period.

Put at its simplest, orchids are herbaceous perennial plants.
This point may need emphasising, as such is the mystique that surrounds orchids that it is easy to forget that in most respects they differ little from other plants that are grown in gardens.

Orchis is a Greek word meaning testicle – a reference to the shape of orchid root tubers. In folk medicine orchids have widely been held to have aphrodisiac powers. The plant family Orchidaceae is one of the largest on the planet, comprising some 25,000 species. They are remarkably widespread, being found in all continents apart from Antarctica.
The majority, however, occur in mainly wet areas in tropical and sub-tropical regions.

How orchids grow
In temperate parts of the world, orchids are rooted in the ground like other plants – in other words they are terrestrial. Nearer the equator, however, they tend to grow epiphytically – on trees (epiphytic comes from the Greek epi, meaning upon, and phyton, meaning plant). Their roots are exposed to air and light, and their main function is to fix the plant to the host.
They are not parasites, and do not derive nutrients from the host plant. Nutrients needed to support growth – derived from bird droppings and decaying plant material – are carried in the more or less constant rain that washes over the plant. There are also a few species that are found growing among rocks and these are referred to as lithophytes. Nearly all the hybrid orchids that are grown in collections today have been bred from epiphytic species.
Terrestrial orchids have rhizomes, swollen stems that grow sideways, or tubers, swollen roots that store nutrients. Epiphytic orchids can grow in one of two ways. Sympodial orchids grow horizontally, producing rhizomes. In most cases, these carry swollen bulb-like structures called pseudobulbs, from which the leaves and flowers appear. These are storage organs that allow the plant to go dormant for short periods. New pseudobulbs are produced each season. After three or four years, the top growth dies back, but the old pseudobulb remains. In the wild, sympodial orchids grow in rainforest at sea level or low altitudes.
Monopodial orchids, found in dense, steamy rainforest at higher altitudes, have upward-growing stems. In the wild, they clamber up through dense jungle to reach the tree canopy.

How orchids are named
Plant names often baffle gardeners. And even gardeners with some experience find that orchid names seem not to follow the conventional rules. In the plant kingdom orchids represent something of a unique case in this respect. It's worth unpicking what orchid names represent, however, as they offer a key to how each plant has evolved, its parentage and even, in some cases, how best to grow it.

Naturally occurring orchids
Along with all other living things, orchids are classified according to the binomial system. This breaks down the family (in this case Orchidaceae) into various distinct genera (singular genus), each styled in italic type and capitalised – eg Phalaenopsis. Genera usually consist of a number of species, all botanically distinct though related to each other. Their names are styled in italic and sometimes convey some information about the plant. Phalaenopsis sumatrana,

for instance, is found in Sumatra. Species can vary in their natural habitat, and so are sometimes divided further into subspecies, varietas or forma. Pleione formosana var. alba, for example, is a naturally occurring white form of P. formosana.

Hybrids

Within the plant world closely related species can sometimes interbreed, resulting in interspecific hybrids. Hybrids are always more robust and have bigger flowers than naturally occurring plants.

Orchids are unusual in that certain species can be crossed outside the genus to produce intergeneric hybrids. The progeny can be further crossed with another species, backcrossed with one of the parents (to consolidate a certain feature), or can be crossed with yet another genus. Orchid hybrids can involve as man as 20 separate species from anything up to 9 genera (bi- tri- or multigeneric, depending on the number). These genera are of course artificial, and their names are often a combination of the names of the parents. For example, Brassocattleya is a cross of Brassavola and Cattleya and Brassolaeliocattleya involves Brassavola, Laelia and Cattleya. Some of the names honour a particular breeder or grower, for instance Wilsonara and Colmanara. Orchids have the most systematically maintained stud book of any group of plants, and all new hybrids that are sold commercially are registered in the International Orchid Register. It is therefore possible to establish the lineage of any hybrid. Extensive work by breeders has created a huge range of orchids with flowers of unparalleled glamour and extended flowering season. Many of the modern phalaenopsis,

top: Monopodial orchids such as this vanda have an upright habit of growth.
bottom: Sympodial orchids spread laterally. The plant shown here is Lepanthopsis astrophora.

for example, are more or less permanently in bloom. Ease of cultivation is yet another bonus, as many of the hybrids are far less exacting in their requirements than the species.

Alliances Interbreeding has resulted in large groups of plants of roughly similar habit and cultivation needs. Many of the hybrid orchids are, depending on their parentage, organised into alliances. The odontoglossum alliance comprises not only Odontoglossum itself but related genera such as Cochlioda, Miltonia, Mitoniopsis, Oncidium and the artificial genera created by interbreeding.
The cattleya alliance includes Cattleya, Laelia, Sophronitis and Brassavola.
The phalaenopsis alliance involves Phalaenopsis and the related Doritis and Ascocentrum.

Grexes When you cross two different plants the resulting batch of seedlings is a grex, or hybrid group. Grex names are styled in roman. For example, crossing Phragmipedium longifolium with P. schlimii produced Phragmipedium Sedenii. It is possible to cross a grex with a species, or another grex. For example, Cymbidium New Dimension was created by crossing C. Mavourneen with C. Sussex Moor. Conventionally, the pollen parent – the male – is listed before the seed parent. Crosses made the other way will yield different results.
If any particular seedling within a grex shows a certain distinction, it can be given a name of its own, styled in roman and placed within single inverted commas. Cymbidium New Dimension, for example, is a grex of mainly green-flowered plants while Cymbidium New Dimension 'Standard White' has white flowers.

Orchid flowers

Orchid flowers show astonishing diversity in structure. What is immediately apparent is that, like a human face, they are symmetrical only in the vertical plane, not top to bottom. Look closely at an unopened bud and you will see that it is made up of three segments, the sepals. As the flower opens, these flare out in a triangular arrangement at the back of the flower to reveal three inner petals. Two of these spread out horizontally and are symmetrical. The central petal, which often projects downwards, has a different shape and is usually referred to as the lip. This functions as a landing stage for pollinating insects. In the so-called slipper orchids, the lip is modified into a pouch.
Looking at an orchid flower from the front, the upper sepal – also referred to as dorsal – is visible at the back of the flower, but often shows different coloration to the true petals. The other two sepals can be masked by the petals, but are often highly visible.

Flower markings

The flower markings that so delight us growers have evolved to attract pollinating insects. Male insects are attracted to dark rather than light colours. Many orchids, though predominantly light, are heavily spotted with darker colours. Yellow also seems to appeal to insects, and this colour is often seen in the lips of certain orchids. The strong lines found on some flowers guide insects to the reproductive parts.

opposite: top left: Cattleyas have flamboyant flowers, usually with ruffled and crimped petal edges. top right: The flowers of Cirrhopetalum picturatum have distinctive, elongated sepals. bottom left: Slipper orchids are so-called because the flowers have inflated, slipper-like lips. bottom right: Odontoglossums show the greatest diversity of any orchid group, many having strikingly marked flowers.

growing orchids at home

So you want to grow orchids, or perhaps have recently bought one? There is a plethora of books on the library shelves, some highly specialised – this is, after all, a huge subject. But many of the orchids on sale today are intended for growing as houseplants, a role they fulfil superbly, and, provided you follow a few simple rules, they are extremely easy to maintain.

Caring for your orchids

If you've done your preliminary research and invested in some fine specimens, you will naturally want to know how best to care for them. Rather than discarding an orchid once the display has finished, follow the advice given here and you will have a plant that keeps on growing lustily and flowering profusely for years to come.

Where to buy orchids

You can buy orchids in garden centres, florists and sometimes supermarkets and department stores. These plants are always sold in flower.

The most popular plants are phalaenopsis, which are easy to produce commercially, flower over a long period and thrive in conditions that wouldn't suit a lot of other flowering plants – namely, a dry, centrally heated living room with a relatively low light level. Although such plants might be labelled as 'phalaenopsis', that's about all the information you will be given. You won't be told the hybrid group or the specific cultivar name. This is fine if you are just buying the plant as a gift or as an alternative to cut flowers. But once you become hooked on these plants, you are likely to become more selective.

A good way of sourcing new plants is to go to plant fairs and flower shows where orchid growers may be exhibiting. Good as the range may be, they are likely to be selling only mature plants that are in flower. For the widest choice, visit an orchid nursery. Orchid growers advertise in the gardening press, but an Internet search will help locate nearby outlets.

At a nursery you can buy not only mature flowering plants, but also smaller specimens for growing on to flowering size. New, unflowered seedlings may also be available. While there may be no description of the flowers available, you will have a rough idea of what to expect from the parentage of the seedling.

At a specialist nursery, you are also likely to find rare species and hybrids that have not been propagated in quantity and hence are not freely available through other sources. These days you can also buy orchids over the Internet, even on eBay.

Obviously you should be as cautious when buying orchids online as you would be buying any other commodity, and it's best to stick to reputable suppliers.

Always beware of buying rare species that may have been collected in the wild – an illegal practice. You needn't worry about buying plants via mail order, however, as they travel extremely well, provided they are packaged correctly.

Nowadays orchids are not prohibitively expensive, but you can still spread the cost by clubbing together with friends and buying a collection, which should have a lower unit cost.

Cultivation

Orchids are mainly tropical plants. To grow them successfully in the home or conservatory, it's necessary to replicate the conditions enjoyed by their wild ancestors to a certain extent – though one of the goals of extensive hybridisation has been to raise their tolerance level, with the result that many of the hybrids are much less exacting than the species.

We are used to thinking in terms of a cycle of four seasons – spring, summer, autumn and winter. Comparing the winter and summer solstices, there is a wide divergence in day length.

Temperature

Orchids are often classified according to their temperature requirements. (The plant pages indicate the appropriate range for each orchid.)

Warm-growing orchids are species that occur in tropical regions at sea level or low altitude. They need a minimum night-time temperature of 20-24°C (68-75°F) and a maximum daytime temperature of 30-33°C (86-91°F).

Intermediate-growing orchids are found in mid-range altitudes and need a minimum night-time temperature of 14-19°C (57-66°F) and a maximum daytime temperature of 30-33°C (86-91°F).

Cool-growing orchids occur in mid-range to high altitudes in the tropics. They need a minimum night-time temperature of 10-13°C (50-55°F) and a maximum daytime temperature of 21-24°C (70-75°F).

These requirements are general and in certain cases have to be expanded. Cymbidiums, for example, which are generally cool growing, need a period of fluctuating temperatures in late summer to autumn to initiate flower production. To achieve this, stand the plants outdoors in that period to make use of the steep temperature drops at night.

There is a contingent differential in temperature across the year, with - at least theoretically - hot summers and cold winters. The closer to the equatorial tropics you go the more this cycle breaks down, and, in such regions (home to many orchids), it is more practical to divide the year into two - a dry and a wet season. Across the year, there is a narrower temperature range and a less steep fluctuation in light levels as daylength evens out.

This all affects plant growth. Close to the equator, plants can be more or less permanently in growth. In practice, most orchids experience periods of growth and dormancy, though they may be dormant for a much shorter period than plants found nearer the polar regions. Managing dormancy can be an important part of orchid care.

Light

Orchids like a nice, even light across the year. In temperate regions, light levels are generally too high in summer and too low in winter. A light position near a window is suitable for most orchids, but this should be shaded in summer, when the sun is strongest, or there is a danger that the plant can scorch. A light blind or curtain over the glass will filter the light. In winter, orchids should be in full light.

Containers

Many orchids grow happily in ordinary plant pots, but it is important that they are free draining. Plastic is usually a better choice than terracotta, which tends to hold on to moisture. Orchids are usually sold in clear plastic pots, which have the advantage over conventional pots of allowing the roots access to light. These can be stood in plant pot holders while the plants are in flower to increase their aesthetic appeal.

You can also use special orchid baskets, which

Mounting on bark

Bearing in mind the way orchids grow in the wild, you might reasonably decide to dispense with containers altogether. Many epiphytic orchids will grow tied to pieces of bark, which can either be pinned to a wall or suspended horizontally from the ceiling. Alternatively, attach them to the branches of large indoor plants such as Ficus or Monstera. This is an effective way to display some of the daintier species as well as hybrids that have a naturally pendent habit, such as some of the dendrobiums.

To reduce possible abrasion if you are mounting an orchid on bark, place a cushion of coconut fibre between the plant and the bark then tie the orchid on with a length of fishing line, wire or horticultural string.

are usually made of plastic and sold in a range of sizes. Conventional hanging baskets are suitable for large plants. Baskets, which have to be suspended from above, are ideal for displaying orchids that have a pendent habit.

As a general rule, containers should provide a tight fit for the roots.

Staking

It is advisable to stake the flower stems of many hybrid orchids. Breeding has produced plants with large flowers, and these can weigh down the stems that carry them. Insert canes next to flower stems as they emerge, taking care not to damage the root system.

opposite, clockwise from top left: Plant clips and ties, plastic orchid baskets, a clear plastic orchid pot, canes for staking.

Attach the stems to the canes as they grow, either using special plastic clips, wire tires or short lengths of horticultural string.
Species orchids and those with naturally arching, pendent stems do not need staking.

Composts

Orchid composts are quite unlike conventional potting composts.
In fact, it is better to think of them as growing mediums rather than as compost. Orchids need a free flow of oxygen and water around their roots, so the compost is really no more than a stabilising medium in which the roots can lodge - delivering nutrients to the plant is not its prime function.
It is critical that any medium used for growing orchids is open and free draining. Most epiphytic orchid composts are based on bark chips. Alternatives include coconut chips, rocks, lava rock, crumbled charcoal or wooden chips. Vermiculite or perlite can be added to any of these to improve aeration. Polystyrene chips are useful for lining the base of a pot.
Adding rockwool is sometimes recommended for cymbidiums and some other orchids that benefit from firm potting. This helps the compost retain water.
Composts for terrestrial orchids are finer grade. These are also suitable for epiphytic orchids with fine root systems.

Watering

Most orchids should be watered freely when they are in active growth, as often as once or twice a week. Reduce watering when the plants are resting in winter. Depending on the species or hybrid group, water to keep the compost just moist or allow the compost to dry out completely.
Tap water can be used, but if you live in a hard water area you may prefer to boil the water first to eliminate traces of calcium that can leave a white deposit. Allow the water to stand until it is at room temperature. Water freely and allow the pots to drain completely. Water around each plant, not directly over it. Never water onto pseudobulbs, as any trapped water can lead to rotting.

Humidity

In view of their rainforest origins, it follows that you need to maintain an appropriate humidity level for your orchids.
In the tropics, humidity has the effect of lowering air temperature. In a home many tropical orchids - or their hybrids - are happy growing at lower temperatures than they would in the wild, so creating a comparable level of humidity is not necessary. Increasing the humidity in summer can be perceived as a means of lowering the temperature.
If you are growing your orchids in a glasshouse or conservatory with a hard floor, hose down the floor every morning in summer. If your orchids are tropical rather than subtropical, repeat this process in the late afternoon or early evening.
You should also spray the plants twice daily. In winter, damping down is not usually necessary.
In a living room, mist orchids once or twice a day in spring and summer. (There are a few orchids that should not be misted - details are given on the plant pages.) You can also create a humid atmosphere around plants by standing the pots on humidity trays containing pebbles or expanded clay pellets. Top the trays up with water as necessary.
Orchids are companiable plants. If you grow a number of different types with similar cultivation needs, group them together. This helps maintain humidity around the plants and creates the appropriate microclimate.

opposite, clockwise from top left: Rockwool, polystyrene chips, a coarse, bark-based epiphytic orchid compost, vermiculite, terrestrial orchid compost, expanded clay pellets.

Feeding

If you want your orchids to grow lustily and produce masses of flowers, you obviously need to feed them. Compared to many other plants, however, they have a low nutrient requirement and overfeeding is counterproductive. It actually increases their susceptibility to many diseases. You can buy special orchid fertilisers. Some are held in phials that are inserted directly into orchid pots so that fertiliser is regularly supplied as a drip (see picture, right). Others have to be diluted and watered around the roots. It is not essential to buy special fertilisers, however. Garden fertilisers such as tomato food or hanging basket fertiliser can be substituted, but applied at a quarter to half the recommended strength. Both these fertilisers are high in potassium, a trace element that encourages free-flowering.

Actually, although many growers feed their orchids by means of a drip or root drench, there are others who doubt the efficacy of delivering a liquid feed in this manner – and obviously this method is unsuitable for orchids mounted on bark. All orchid composts are free draining, and it stands to reason that the majority of the dose will leach through, wasting a large proportion of the nutrients. A more effective method of feeding orchids,

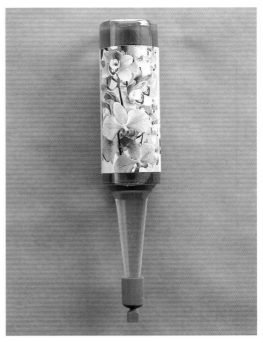

Orchid fertiliser in a phial.

therefore and the only method of applying fertiliser to bark-mounted plants – is to spray on the product as a foliar feed.

Generally you should feed orchids every three to four weeks from spring to summer, although a few species do have different needs (the plant pages provide details of these). Reduce feeding in late summer to autumn. Plants should not be fed in winter, when they are resting.

Repotting

Although many orchids cymbidiums especially seem positively to thrive when their roots are constricted in a pot, there usually comes a point when it is essential to repot. Some plants virtually climb out of their pots, or their roots seem to flow over the sides. Repotting offers a good opportunity to refresh a plant. You can either repot a plant into a larger pot or split it up to make smaller plants (see Propagation, pages 22–27), a process that allows you to cut away any dead or dormant parts of the plant. Repot in spring, just as the plant is coming into growth, or immediately after flowering.

- Slide the plant from its container and shake off the old compost. Cut back any dead roots and any other dead or dormant parts of the plant. Place the plant in its new container so that it is not in the middle – as you would do with most plants – but with the oldest part of the plant against the rim of the container. The young part will then grow into the fresh compost.
- Hold the plant in position with one hand and feed fresh compost or other potting medium in with the other. Use a cane to poke this around the roots and shake the container to settle it around them. Water the plant well.

Common problems

Orchids, despite their exotic origins, are no more vulnerable to pests and diseases than other plants. Like all living things to a certain extent they adapt to the prevalent conditions, and it's a sudden change – such as a widely fluctuating temperature or water supply – that is most likely to be the cause of any lapse
in health. Replicating the ambient conditions they would enjoy in the wild reduces the incidence of problems.

Keeping a close eye on your plants is the key to success. All plant parts should be firm, pseudobulbs especially. Look out for signs of fresh growth in early spring - if the tips of aerial roots turn green, for instance - then step up the watering and also begin your feeding regime.

Points to consider

■ All plants grown under cover - whether in the home, conservatory or in a greenhouse - are susceptible to certain pests and diseases. This is because it is impossible to replicate the diverse eco-system found in nature that ensures a healthy balance between pests
and their natural predators. The closed environment that you'll be growing the plants in actually favours the proliferation of particular pests and diseases.

■ If you just want to freshen up your orchids, place them outdoors during mild, damp weather. This is a particularly useful strategy in spring, when you want to perk plants up after their winter dormancy. Failing that - if you live in a flat, for instance - stand your orchids in the shower periodically and give them a good drench of cold water.

■ Some orchids can be kept outdoors throughout the summer, which is a highly effective method of keeping pests and diseases at bay. Not only do orchids appreciate the fresh air, but the livelier eco-system outdoors ensures that pests seldom multiply to harmful levels. Keep an eye out for slugs, however. They will eat holes in all but the toughest leaves.

■ Prevention is better than cure and it pays to be vigilant. For example, say you are growing several orchids in proximity. If you spot a problem on one of them, put it in quarantine while you deal with the problem to lessen the chances of it spreading to the other plants.

■ Routine maintenance should involve the prompt removal of dead flowers, as dead material tends to attract fungal spores. You should also remove dead leaves - or any that are showing signs of dieback or excessive yellowing.

■ Repotting as and when necessary provides a good opportunity to cut out and discard any old, withered pseudobulbs and any dead roots (see box, opposite).

■ If you do encounter any of the problems that are detailed overleaf, make sure that you deal with them as swiftly as possible to ensure the health of your orchid collection.

Pests

Most gardeners will be familiar with the following pests, but some are of tropical origin so tend only to be found on plants grown under cover. Hence the value of putting plants outdoors whenever possible.

If you find you need to tackle plant pests in the home, it's also worth keeping a lookout for ants. Ants do not in themselves cause significant damage to plants, but they are attracted to the sticky honeydew that many pests excrete. In the course of their wanderings they will carry the eggs of the pests to other plants, potentially compounding your problems. So as well as carrying out the measures suggested here, put down some ant poison near the plants – or near the nest, if there already is one and you can track it down – to avoid any infestations.

The following are among the commonest orchid pests.

Greenfly	Probably the most common of all insect pests, these tiny, winged green aphids often enter the home via open windows in spring and summer. They feed on young growth, and their sticky excreta will attract sooty mould (see diseases, opposite). Control: Spray the plants with a strong jet of water – best done outdoors – as this is usually sufficient to dislodge the pest.
Red spider mite	This is an all too common pest of plants grown under glass. The mite itself is tiny, and tends to be active on the undersides of leaves. It is betrayed by fine silk webs on the leaves. Infested leaves show a silvery white mottling, which in itself attracts such fungal diseases as sooty mould (see opposite). Control: Mist your orchids regularly, as the pest proliferates in a hot, dry atmosphere. Spray infested plants with an insecticidal soap. In a greenhouse, the pest can be controlled by the parasitic Phytoseiulus persimilis (generally only sold via mail order).
Scale insects	Scale insects are tiny insects that are covered by a hard or waxy shell. Like barnacles they cling to the undersides of leaves, on which they feed. They go unnoticed easily until their excreta (honeydew), which drips down onto lower plant parts, makes the plant sticky, attracting such fungal problems as sooty mould (see diseases, opposite). Control: Most insecticides are ineffective, as the pests are protected by their shells. The best method is to use a stiff brush, such as an old toothbrush, dipped in an insectidal solution to scrub the scales off the leaves. Several campaigns may be necessary to eliminate the pest entirely.
Slugs and enter snails	Rarely found in the home, these molluscs are common in the garden and can greenhouses and sometimes conservatories. They cause most damage in spring, when plant growth is soft. The wounds they create render the soft tissue exposed vulnerable to disease. Trim back any damaged material with a sharp knife and dust the cut surfaces with a fungicidal powder. Control: Gardeners use slug pellets or traps or pick the molluscs off plants by hand. Possibly the most effective method from the orchid grower's point of view is the attaching of metal strips around the edges of pots, which deliver an electric shock to the molluscs. Tip: If you do summer your orchids outdoors, check the bases of the pots daily and flick off any slugs that may be hiding underneath.

Vine weevil	Increasingly the scourge of gardeners, this is a pest that favours pot plants. Plants that spend their summers outdoors are the likeliest to fall victim to it. The adults are winged black beetles that are active in summer, occasionally eating the topgrowth of plants. It's the creamy white grubs that cause most damage, however. The females lay their eggs around the plant and the emerging grubs tunnel downwards to feed on plant roots. You may not realise you have a problem until you repot in spring, only to discover the plant has no roots left. Alternatively, the plant may simply collapse. Control: The most effective method of controlling this particular pest is to water with a parasitic nematode, either Heterorhabditis megidis or Steinernema carpocapsae, which are available via mail order. When repotting, check carefully for grubs. If you have had problems with the pest before, hold the roots under running water to flush out any eggs and repot in fresh compost.

Diseases

Plant diseases are caused by fungi, bacteria and viruses – fungi are the most common. Fungi proliferate where the air is damp and stagnant; conditions of exactly the type that can build up where plants are crowded together and air circulation is reduced with less water lost through transpiration. Ventilating plants, or just standing them outdoors for short periods, can help prevent fungi taking a hold. Bacteria can only enter plants through their natural openings or through wounds. Viruses are more of a mystery, but are often transferred by insect carriers that introduce the virus into the plant during the course of their feeding activities. The following are some of the most common orchid diseases.

Black	This is a fungal disease that affects pseudobulbs, usually as a result of overwatering. The pseudobulb pseudobulbs turn brown or black and leaves can turn yellow. Cymbidiums seem particularly rot vulnerable to this. Control: Isolate affected plants and drench them with a fungicide. Cut off affected parts and treat the cuts with a fungicide. Check that the compost is free draining: repotting in fresh compost is advisable. Really badly affected plants are best thrown away.
Cymbidium	This virus commonly affects cymbidiums, but can also appear on other types of orchid. The mosaic virus disease is probably spread by aphids, but can also take hold during the propagation process. The first sign is a white flecking on the leaves, which later turns black. Flowering can also often be impaired. Control: There's no known cure for this problem, and affected plants should be discarded. Any plant you think may be showing signs of the disease should be quarantined from all others until you've ascertained whether it really is carrying the disease or not. If you've had a problem with this virus, take particular care when propagating that any cutting tools are clean.
Sooty mould	The appearance of sooty mould – a black powdery deposit on the uppersides of leaves is an indication that you've neglected to deal with some pest, whose sticky excreta has encouraged the fungus to take a hold. Control: If only a few leaves are affected, cut them off and treat the cut surfaces with a fungicide. If the leaves are very tough and hard, it may be possible to scrub off the mould with a stout toothbrush dipped in a fungicidal solution.

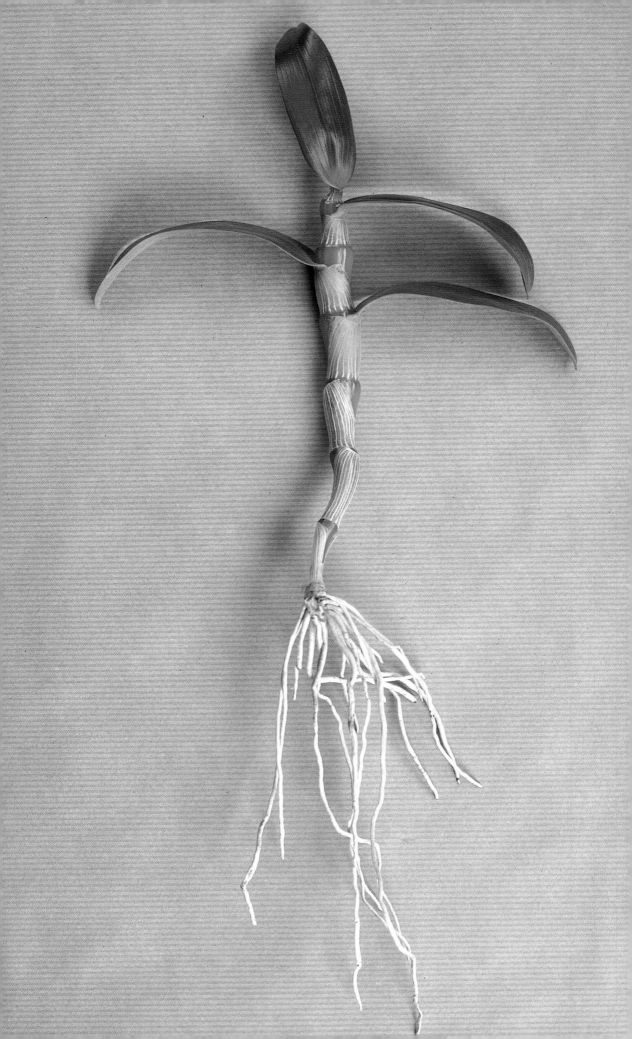

propagation

In commerce, new orchid hybrids are constantly being introduced and older ones - inevitably - can fall by the wayside. If you have a particularly valued plant keep up stocks of it, both for yourself and for other enthusiasts. This ensures that the plant will never totally disappear from cultivation.

Depending on their growth habit, in time orchids can become unwieldy plants with large amounts of dead-looking, or at least dormant, material. Propagating results in a certain number of fresher, more productive and manageable plants, and also enables you to breathe life into apparently moribund plant material.

Commercially, orchids are often propagated by 'meristem culture', a micropropagation technique that relies on laboratory conditions for success. It's this technological advance that has brought down the price of orchids to growers. But there are a number of other techniques that are well within the capabilities of amateur growers. Seed, however, is not among them.

Orchid seed is dust-like and, like meristem culture, requires laboratory conditions for success.

The methods available to amateur growers are essentially vegetative, and the new plants produced will be identical to the parent plant. As you start propagating, bear in mind that although orchid propagation by the methods suggested here is simple and reliable, it may take several years before the new plants reach flowering size.

Practical propagating tips

■ Use a sharp knife or secateurs when cutting orchids for propagation. Scissors can be used for very small plants and for removing keikis (see page 27).

■ A closed propagating case can be useful to maintain a humid environment that keeps cuttings alive and encourages rooting, but is by no means always essential. As an alternative, tent the cuttings in a plastic bag.

■ However you root your cuttings, you need to guard against fungal infections. To do this, remove the covering regularly and treat the cuttings with a fungicide.

Division

Sympodial orchids can be propagated by simple division. You can divide your plants when they have become congested – many get to the point when they appear to be virtually clambering out of the pot. Divide either in spring or immediately after flowering.

Slide the plant out of its container and shake the roots free of compost. Depending on how congested the plant is, either tease it into sections by hand, or use a sharp knife or secateurs to cut it into sections.

Each section should have at least three or four live growing points – in other words, areas that are leaf-bearing or obviously about to push out new leaves. Cut off any pseudobulbs without topgrowth. Old, shrivelled ones are best discarded, but firm, plump ones – known as backbulbs – can be coaxed back into life using the method described opposite.

Trim back any dead or damaged roots.

Pot up the divisions in pots that will comfortably accommodate them. The oldest part of the plant should be in contact with the edge of the pot, leaving room for the youngest part to grow outwards and fill the pot. Fill the pot with compost. If you are using a coarse compost, such as bark chips, use a cane to firm the material around the roots. Water the plant well in order to settle the compost around the roots and top up with more compost as necessary.

Owing to their habit of growth, monopodial orchids do not readily lend themselves to division, but sometimes produce keikis, as is described on page 27.

Propagating from backbulbs

Wrap firm backbulbs in damp moss and pot these individually into small containers that will hold the moss in place. Alternatively, pot them individually into small pots of the same compost that is recommended for the parent. Keep them warm and humid, ideally in a closed propagating case, in a bright spot but shaded from direct sunlight.

New growth should appear at the base of the pseudobulbs after approximately six weeks. Once this growth is about 5cm (2in) high, remove the pots from the propagator, water twice weekly and feed every four to six weeks while in active growth. Pot on six months later into pots that are only slightly larger, then continue to repot at six-monthly intervals until a new pseudobulb has formed. The new plants can then be treated as adult specimens.

top right: A congested orchid.

bottom right: Cut the plant into sections, each with three or four active growing points.

Stem cuttings

Stem cuttings can be used for dendrobiums and other orchids that have cane-like stems, such as some of the epidendrums. Suitable stems for cutting are dormant – in other words leafless – but they should have bright green nodes (the joints on the stem from where the leaves have been shed).

In spring, remove old, dormant canes from the plant and cut into sections with a sharp knife or secateurs. Each section should have one or two nodes. Dust the ends of the cuttings with sulphur or other fungicidal powder to prevent rotting.

Plunge the cuttings up to half their length in pots or trays of orchid compost. Alternatively, lay the cuttings horizontally on shallow trays of moss. Place the cuttings in a closed propagating case. Keep them in a bright place but shaded from direct sun.

New growth should appear from the nodes after two or three months. Pot up the new plants individually and grow them on in the same way as you would adult plants.

Tip: If your dendrobium is of the D. biggibum type, only the upper portions of the stem provide suitable cuttings material.

top: A dendrobium stem cut into pieces ready for propagating.
middle: A stem cutting laid on moss.
bottom: Cuttings can also be potted vertically in orchid compost.

Keikis

Some orchids, notably some of the dendrobiums, produce so-called adventitious growths. These are virtually complete plants with ready-formed root systems growing on the upper portions of the plant. They are usually referred to as 'keikis' and can be removed and grown on to form new plants. When the keikis' root systems are well developed, propagate by removing them carefully from the plant – either by hand or with the cautious use of a sharp knife or scissors. Pot up the keikis in standard orchid compost as recommended for the parent type. No special aftercare is required as they can be treated as adult plants straightaway. Monopodial orchids, such as Phalaenopsis, also occasionally produce keikis – though less frequently than Dendrobium – usually as a result of stress or inappropriate cultivation. You can encourage keikis by coating the nodes with keiki paste, available from orchid nurseries.

Do be aware that keikis are generally produced at the expense of flowers.

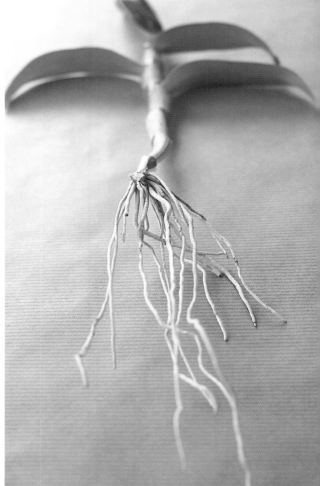

top: A keiki still attached to its parent plant – in this case, a dendrobium.
bottom: What a keiki should look like once it has been carefully removed from the parent.

cattleyas

The term cattleya embraces not only Cattleya itself but a number of related genera native to tropical South America. Cattleyas are the orchids with the huge, glamorous, richly coloured flowers. But hybrids with smaller flowers, often of jewel-like brilliance, are not to be overlooked. The leaves are also distinctive, thick and leathery, and lower portions of stems are often wrapped in a papery sheath. The flowers do not last so long as those of some other orchids (a mere three weeks), and the plants need a little more care than some other groups to encourage them to flower which often occurs when the plant is resting.

Brassolaeliocattleya Founders Circle

The evergreen genera Brassavola, Laelia and Cattleya were involved in creating this trigeneric hybrid.
Its parents are also brassolaeliocattleyas, Blc.
Fortune and Green-heart Stewart Inc. Founders Circle was registered in 1983.

In many ways this is an archetypal cattleya, having flamboyant,fragrant blooms almost 15cm (6in) across and of a warm, luminous violet. The lips are more richly coloured and are marked with yellow on the inside.
Both petals and lips are ruffled at the edges.

The leaves are leathery and almost hard in texture.
When the plant is in full flower take care when watering, as stray drops of water can blemish the flowers easily.

QUICK REFERENCE

PLANT SIZE
Up to 40cm (16in).

NUMBER OF FLOWERS
2 or 3 per stem.

FLOWERING PERIOD
Spring and autumn.

REGULARITY OF FLOWERING
Annually.

HABIT OF GROWTH
Evergreen sympodial orchid with sturdy, cylindrical pseudobulbs.

BEST WAY TO GROW
Grow in a pot of epiphytic orchid compost with added rockwool and vermiculite.

GENERAL CARE
Intermediate growing (min 14-19°C/57-66°F; max 30-33°C/86-91°F). Shade from direct light in summer; full light in winter. Water freely when in full growth and mist daily (do not mist over open flowers). In winter, water only to prevent the compost drying out. Feed every 3 to 4 weeks during the period after flowering.

PROPAGATION
Divide when the plant outgrows its container. Pot up backbulbs separately.

EASE OF CULTIVATION
Some experience required.

Brassolaeliocattleya Malworth

This is a tried and tested hybrid, registered in 1963, that involves Laeliocattlya Charlesworthii and Malvern - the name is a conflation of the two parent grex names. It has been further crossed with other brassolaeliocattleyas to produce a range of hybrids with Malworth as part of the name, such as Malworth Sparkle and Malworth Sunset.

The petals and sepals of this plant are a soft peachy yellow, the lips being a richer salmon pink with that ruffling at the edges that typifies the cattleyas.

A gorgeous flower, up to 15cm (6in) across, and fragrant too - for something comparable, try Brassolaeliocattleya George King 'Serendipity', which shows a similar colouring.

QUICK REFERENCE

PLANT SIZE
Up to 30cm (12in).

NUMBER OF FLOWERS
1 or 2 (occasionally more) per stem.

FLOWERING PERIOD
Spring or autumn.

REGULARITY OF FLOWERING
Annually.

HABIT OF GROWTH
Evergreen sympodial orchid with sturdy, cylindrical pseudobulbs.

BEST WAY TO GROW
Grow in a pot of epiphytic orchid compost with added rockwool and vermiculite.

GENERAL CARE
Intermediate growing (min 14-19ºC/57-66ºF; max 30-33ºC/86-91ºF). Shade from direct light in summer; full light in winter. Water freely when in full growth and mist daily (do not mist over open flowers). In winter, water only to prevent the compost drying out. Feed every 3 to 4 weeks during the period after flowering.

PROPAGATION
Divide when the plant outgrows its container. Pot up backbulbs separately.

EASE OF CULTIVATION
Some experience necessary.

Iwanagaara Appleblossom

A plant of considerable elegance, this intergeneric hybrid resulted from a complex cross of Brassavola x Cattleya x Diacrium x Laelia, which all have their origins in South America. Its immediate parents are Caulaelia Snowflake and Brassolaeliocattleya Orange Nuggett, and it was registered in 1992. It has been used itself as a parent plant to create further hybrids.

The clusters of sweetly scented flowers, which are up to 10cm (4in) across, are blush white flared with pink. The petals are broader than the sepals and have delicately crimped edges.

The lips are pale purplish pink and are heavily stained with yellow within. This particular cattleya thrives on a windowsill.

QUICK REFERENCE

PLANT SIZE
Up to 30cm (12in).

NUMBER OF FLOWERS
2 or 3 per stem.

FLOWERING PERIOD
Spring.

REGULARITY OF FLOWERING
Annually.

HABIT OF GROWTH
Evergreen sympodial orchid that has small pseudobulbs.

BEST WAY TO GROW
Grow in a pot of epiphytic orchid compost with added rockwool and vermiculite.

GENERAL CARE
Intermediate growing (min 14–19ºC/57–66ºF; max 30–33ºC/86–91ºF). Keep shaded from direct sun in summer; full light in winter. Water freely and mist daily when in active growth; reduce watering in winter. Feed every 3 or 4 weeks when in active growth.

PROPAGATION
Divide when the plant outgrows its container; detach dormant backbulbs and pot up separately.

EASE OF CULTIVATION
An easy hybrid to grow and flower.

Laeliocattleya El Cerrito

The laeliocattleyas are bigeneric hybrids of the evergreen genera Laelia and Cattleya, both of which occur in Central and South America. El Cerrito is a primary hybrid that resulted from a cross of two species, Laelia flava, from southeast Brazil, and the variable Cattleya aurantica, from Central America. It was registered in 1962.

The flowers, which are up to 5cm (2in) across and carried in small clusters, are a pure, rich tangerine orange, with petals and sepals that are delicately recurving and exquisitely formed, trumpet-like lips. They are set off well by the thick, substantial leaves. The plant's mixed parentage means that it will tolerate a wider temperature range than some orchids, but it will probably do best in the higher range listed opposite. When the plant is resting hold back on the watering, giving just enough to prevent the pseudobulbs from shrivelling.

QUICK REFERENCE

PLANT SIZE
Up to 45cm (18in).

NUMBER OF FLOWERS
3 or more per stem.

FLOWERING PERIOD
Spring or summer.

REGULARITY OF FLOWERING
Annually.

HABIT OF GROWTH
Evergreen sympodial orchid with elongated pseudobulbs.

BEST WAY TO GROW
Grow in a pot or basket filled with epiphytic orchid compost.

GENERAL CARE
Cool growing (min 10-13ºC/50-55ºF; max 21-24ºC/ 70-75ºF) to intermediate growing (min 14-19ºC/57-66ºF; max 30-33ºC/ 86-91ºF). Shade from hot sun in summer; full light in winter. Water freely when in active growth and mist daily. Water less in winter. Feed every 3 or 4 weeks during the period after flowering.

PROPAGATION
Divide when the plant outgrows its container, and pot up dormant backbulbs separately.

EASE OF CULTIVATION
Some experience of orchid cultivation is desirable.

Potinara Thais de Valec

Potinaras are derived from crosses between four evergreen genera from Central and South America - Brassavola, Cattleya, Laelia and Sophronitis - and are named after the French orchid grower M. Potin. Thais de Valec is a new hybrid, bred from Potinara Farrell d'Or and Laeliocattleya Trick or Treat. Most potinaras produce flowers of strong, clear colour, usually yellow or red, and this hybrid is no exception. It was registered in 2001.

The heads of bright orange flowers, which are unmarked by contrasting colours, are 12cm (5in) across, making them smaller than those of the more flamboyant cattleyas.
This perhaps betrays the plant's sophronitis genes which are also indicated by its compact habit. The lips show a slightly richer colour and have appealingly ruffled edges.
The centres of the lips fade to a rich near yellow.

QUICK REFERENCE

PLANT SIZE
Up to 35cm (14in).

NUMBER OF FLOWERS
Up to 5 or more per cluster.

FLOWERING PERIOD
Flowers can be produced at any time of the year.

REGULARITY OF FLOWERING
Intermittent.

HABIT OF GROWTH
Evergreen sympodial orchid with stout pseudobulbs.

BEST WAY TO GROW
Grow in a pot containing a coarse epiphytic compost. This plant tolerates being potbound.

GENERAL CARE
Cool growing (min 10-13ºC/50-55ºF; max 21-24ºC/70-75ºF). Shade from direct light in summer; full light in winter. Water freely when in full growth in spring and summer and mist daily; reduce watering in winter. Feed every 3 to 4 weeks when the plant is growing strongly, except when in flower.

PROPAGATION
Divide when the plant outgrows its container. Pot up backbulbs separately.

EASE OF CULTIVATION
Potinaras are easy to grow and bring into flower.

Sophrolaeliocattleya Jeanne Wilson

This is a trigeneric hybrid involving Cattleya, Laelia and the smaller Sophronitis, genes from which have produced plants that are more compact than some of the other cattleyas. Its parents are the complex hybrid Sophrolaeliocattleya Kauai Starbright and a species from eastern Brazil, Sophronitis cernua. It was registered in 1987.

The flowers, which are up to 6.5cm (21/2in) across, are of great elegance. Narrow, pointed and gently recurving, the petals and sepals are a rich cherry red. The lips are marked with a deep creamy yellow at the base.

QUICK REFERENCE

PLANT SIZE
Up to 30cm (12in).

NUMBER OF FLOWERS
2 or 3 per stem.

FLOWERING PERIOD
Late winter to spring, but flowering at other times of year is also possible.

REGULARITY OF FLOWERING
Annually.

HABIT OF GROWTH
Evergreen sympodial orchid with elongated pseudobulbs.

BEST WAY TO GROW
Grow in a container of terrestrial (or fine-grade epiphytic) orchid compost.

GENERAL CARE
Intermediate growing (min 14-19ºC/57-66ºF; max 30-33ºC/86-91ºF), but tolerant of a lower range. Shade from direct sunlight in summer; full light in winter. Water freely and mist daily when in full growth; reduce watering in winter. Feed every 3 to 4 weeks during the period after flowering.

PROPAGATION
Divide when roots fill the container. Pot up dormant backbulbs individually.

EASE OF CULTIVATION
Some experience required.

coelogynes, encyclias and epidendrums

This section comprises three important and easily grown orchid genera that, however, have not undergone the extensive hybridisation visited upon other groups.

The coelogynes, from tropical Asia, are beautiful plants even when out of flower. Those described here make excellent houseplants. Encyclias and epidendrums, from tropical America, are closely related. All the plants included in this chapter have similar cultivation needs and are tolerant of the usually dry atmospheres found in most houses.

Coelogyne corymbosa

Coelogyne is a genus of some 200 evergreens that hail from India, southeast Asia and the Pacific islands – growing in lowland forests as well as at much higher altitudes. C. corymbosa is found in the Himalaya.

This orchid produces crispy white flowers, up to 5cm (2in) across, on short stems. The lips are prettily patterned with yellow blotches that are edged with orange-red. The sepals are somewhat narrower than the petals, giving the open flower an airy look of great elegance. The flower stems are erect initially, but arch over as they lengthen.

This orchid needs a complete rest in winter, when watering should cease. However, if the pseudobulbs show signs of withering mist them occasionally to keep them plump. The plant is unusual in cultivation, the freely flowering C. cristata being more popular among growers.

QUICK REFERENCE

PLANT SIZE
Up to 20cm (8in).

NUMBER OF FLOWERS
2-4 per stem.

FLOWERING PERIOD
Winter and spring.

REGULARITY OF FLOWERING
Annually.

HABIT OF GROWTH
Evergreen sympodial orchid with rounded, flask-like pseudobulbs.

BEST WAY TO GROW
Grow in a container or hanging basket containing epiphytic orchid compost.

GENERAL CARE
Cool growing (min 10-13ºC/50-55ºF; max 21-24ºC/ 70-75ºF).
Shade from hot sun in summer; full light in winter.
Water freely when in growth in spring and summer and mist daily; keep dry in winter.
Feed every 3 to 4 weeks during the period after flowering.

PROPAGATION
Divide as and when the plant becomes congested; remove dormant backbulbs in mid-spring.

EASE OF CULTIVATION
For more experienced growers only.

Coelogyne cristata

This species is found in Nepal in the eastern Himalaya, growing at high altitudes on the trunks and thick branches of trees or on rocks. It is very popular with orchid enthusiasts and is often grown as a houseplant. Mature plants put on a breathtaking display, as the flowers literally cascade down.

The plant produces arching stems of richly fragrant, snow white flowers – each one 8cm (3in) across. The lips are marked with golden yellow. Cristata means 'crested' and refers to the edges of the petals, which are distinctly ruffled. When in full flower the plant can be twice as wide as it is high.

QUICK REFERENCE

PLANT SIZE
Up to 30cm (12in).

NUMBER OF FLOWERS
3-10 per stem.

FLOWERING PERIOD
A long period from winter to spring.

REGULARITY OF FLOWERING
Annually.

HABIT OF GROWTH
Evergreen sympodial orchid that has rounded pseudobulbs.

BEST WAY TO GROW
Grow in a container or more effectively in a hanging basket containing epiphytic orchid compost.

GENERAL CARE
Cool growing (min 10-13ºC/50-55ºF; max 21-24ºC/ 70-75ºF). Shade from hot sun in summer; full light in winter. Water freely when in growth in spring and summer and mist daily. Keep dry in winter. Feed every 3 to 4 weeks during the growing period after flowering.

PROPAGATION
Divide as and when the plant becomes congested; remove dormant backbulbs in mid-spring.

EASE OF CULTIVATION
One of the easiest species for amateurs to grow, so suitable for beginners.

Coelogyne cristata 'Alba'

This form of Coelogyne cristata (see page 47) is found in India rather than Nepal, though it is in a similar climatic region - with short, cool and dry winters and several months of monsoon rains in summer. That knowledge provides useful clues as to how best to grow it at home.

The distinguishing feature of the plant – and what separates it from the straight species – is its pure white flowers, which open to 8cm (3in) across. The fragrance and white colour have evolvedto attract pollinating insects, in this case moths.

Be sure to place the plant where you can fully appreciate its delicious scent, but give it adequate space - in full flower a mature plant can be twice as wide as it is high.

QUICK REFERENCE

PLANT SIZE
Up to 30cm (12in).

NUMBER OF FLOWERS
3-10 per stem.

FLOWERING PERIOD
A long period from winter to spring.

REGULARITY OF FLOWERING
Annually.

HABIT OF GROWTH
Evergreen sympodial orchid that has rounded pseudobulbs.

BEST WAY TO GROW
Grow in a container or more effectively in a hanging basket containing epiphytic orchid compost.

GENERAL CARE
Cool growing (min 10-13ºC/50-55ºF; max 21-24ºC/ 70-75ºF). Shade from hot sun in summer; full light in winter. Water freely when in growth in spring and summer and mist daily. Keep dry in winter. Feed every 3 to 4 weeks during the growing period after flowering.

PROPAGATION
Divide as and when the plant becomes congested; remove dormant backbulbs in mid-spring.

EASE OF CULTIVATION
One of the easiest species for amateurs to grow, so suitable for beginners.

Encyclia cochleata, syn. Epidendrum cochleatum

One of the few species that regularly finds its way into orchid collections, Encyclia cochleata is an evergreen that is found growing epiphytically in a range from Florida to Venezuela.

The flowers are quite intriguing – rather than conventionally beautiful – having ribbon-like, twisting, pale green sepals and petals. Up to 9cm (3½in) across, they are carried singly or in small clusters on relatively short stems. The lips are reddish purple flushed with yellow-green. However, unlike some other Encyclia species, there is unfortunately no fragrance. E. cochleata has the delightful common names of Cockle orchid and Clamshell orchid. It is also of considerable historic interest, as it was one of the first orchids to find its way into cultivation and is recorded as flowering at Kew as long ago as 1787.

QUICK REFERENCE

PLANT SIZE
Up to 45cm (18in).

NUMBER OF FLOWERS
1–5, or even more, per stem.

FLOWERING PERIOD
At various times throughout the year.

REGULARITY OF FLOWERING
Intermittent.

HABIT OF GROWTH
Evergreen sympodial orchid with pear-shaped pseudobulbs.

BEST WAY TO GROW
Grow in a pot or slatted basket that is filled with epiphytic orchid compost.

GENERAL CARE
Cool growing (min 10-13ºC/50-55ºF; max 21-24ºC/ 70-75ºF). Grow in full light but shade from hot sun. Water freely when in growth and mist daily, but keep dry when dormant in winter. Feed every 3 to 4 weeks when in active growth, except when in flower.

PROPAGATION
Divide when the plant becomes congested and pot up the dormant pseudobulbs individually.

EASE OF CULTIVATION
One of the easiest orchid species to grow and bring into flower, so it is very suitable for beginners.

Epidendrum Ballerina Yellow

Epidendrum is a genus of tall-growing epiphytes from tropical regions of the Americas. The ballerina epidendrums are a group of hybrids derived from E. ibaguense (syn. E. radicans) – Ibagué being a town in Colombia. Sometimes called the fiery reed orchid, this is a variable species from Mexico, south to Argentina. As with all the epidendrums, it is rewarding to grow as it is so seldom without flower.

The flowers are small (up to 5cm/2in across) but they are borne in quantity, in elegant panicles rather like an agapanthus, and the display can last for several months. Individual flowers are worth studying in detail. Though of uniform colour, the lips are attractively fringed at the edges – which is a feature of the genus. Remove the faded flowers singly, as this encourages the panicle to produce further flowering shoots. Though a plant can be more or less permanently in flower, in practice you are likely to have to give the plant a rest during winter (when you can let the compost virtually dry out). There are also white, pink, orange, lettuce green and purple forms. To ensure a long flowering season, maintain even conditions throughout the year.

QUICK REFERENCE

PLANT SIZE
Up to 35cm (14in) when in flower.

NUMBER OF FLOWERS
15 or more per cluster.

FLOWERING PERIOD
No clearly defined flowering season.

REGULARITY OF FLOWERING
An established plant can flower all year.

HABIT OF GROWTH
Evergreen sympodial orchid that has reed-like pseudobulbs.

BEST WAY TO GROW
Grow in a container filled with epiphytic or terrestrial orchid compost.

GENERAL CARE
Intermediate growing (min 14-19ºC/57-66ºF; max 30-33ºC/86-91ºF). Shade from hot sun in summer; full light in winter. Water freely when in full growth and mist daily; water more sparingly in winter, depending on whether the plant is in flower. Feed every 3 to 4 weeks when the plant is in strong growth.

PROPAGATION
Divide when the roots fill the container.

EASE OF CULTIVATION
Easy to grow and bring into flower; an excellent choice for anyone starting an orchid collection.

cymbidiums

The genus Cymbidium does not hybridise so freely as some of the other orchid genera, so, with no intergeneric hybrids, there is a greater uniformity to the plants available. However, breeding has produced plants in different sizes: standard, intermediate and miniature (or compact). Standards are too large for most growers – they can reach up to 1.2m (4ft) in height.

Cymbidiums are among the easiest of orchids to grow, but they can be reluctant to flower every year. To stimulate flowering, they need a steep drop in temperature between day and night at the end of the growing period. The simplest way to achieve this is to put your orchids outdoors in a sheltered spot in late summer, when night temperatures start to fall. Bring them in before any frosts are threatened. Unlike many other orchids, cymbidiums like their roots to be kept fairly cool and damp – in the wild, many grow terrestrially.

Cymbidium Coral Candy

This is a rare hybrid that was registered in 1993, created from a cross between Cymbidium Coral Route and C. Cleo Sherman – the latter being a parent of several new hybrids. Coral Candy is classified as an intermediate cymbidium.

The flowers are relatively large for a cymbidium, up to 10cm (4in) across, and cluster among the grassy leaves towards the ends of the sturdy, upright stems. They are a cool pink, not the hot orange pink that the name might lead you to expect. The lips are marked with irregular maroon blotches, with yellow towards the base. A cool period in late summer through autumn, with fluctuating temperatures between day and night, is necessary to initiate flower production.

QUICK REFERENCE

PLANT SIZE
Up to 60cm (24in).

NUMBER OF FLOWERS
Up to 10 or more per stem.

FLOWERING PERIOD
Autumn and late winter.

REGULARITY OF FLOWERING
Usually annually.

HABIT OF GROWTH
Evergreen sympodial orchid that has pseudobulbs.

BEST WAY TO GROW
Grow in a container that restricts the roots and is filled with epiphytic orchid compost, preferably with added rockwool.

GENERAL CARE
Cool growing (min 10-13ºC/50-55ºF; max 21-24ºC/ 70-75ºF). Shade from direct sun in summer; full light in winter. Water freely when in full growth and mist daily; water less in winter. Feed every 3 to 4 weeks when growing strongly in spring and summer.

PROPAGATION
Divide a congested plant after flowering; pot up dormant pseudobulbs separately.

EASE OF CULTIVATION
An easy orchid for beginners, though not always easy to bring into flower.

Cymbidium Earlisue 'Paddy'

The grex Earlisue, registered in 1993, resulted from crossing Cymbidium Sue with C. Trigo Royale. It is classified as an intermediate cymbidium, referring to the size of the plant - average - not the temperature requirement. 'Paddy' is a selected form, others include 'White Pearl'.

The substantial, waxy flowers are pure ivory white, with yellow and maroon markings inside the lips. Generously proportioned at up to 10cm (4in) across, they are clustered tightly on the upright stems.

To ensure flower production, keep the plant cool in late summer and through autumn.

QUICK REFERENCE

PLANT SIZE
Up to 60cm (24in).

NUMBER OF FLOWERS
Up to 10 or more per stem.

FLOWERING PERIOD
Early to mid-winter.

REGULARITY OF FLOWERING
Usually annually, but can be reluctant without a cool period during late summer-autumn.

HABIT OF GROWTH
Evergreen sympodial orchid that has pseudobulbs.

BEST WAY TO GROW
Grow in a container that restricts the roots and is filled with epiphytic orchid compost, preferably with added rockwool.

GENERAL CARE
Cool growing (min 10-13ºC/50-55ºF; max 21-24ºC/ 70-75ºF). Shade from direct sun in summer; full light in winter. Water freely when in full growth and mist daily; water less in winter. Feed every 3 to 4 weeks when growing strongly in spring and summer.

PROPAGATION
Divide a congested plant after flowering; pot up dormant pseudobulbs separately.

EASE OF CULTIVATION
An easy orchid for beginners, though not always easy to bring into flower.

Cymbidium eburneum

This Cymbidium species, which is found growing epiphytically in damp forest regions of the Himalaya, northern Burma and southwest China, is rare in cultivation. Though rather shy to flower, it makes up for this in the outstanding fragrance of its blooms.

In the wild, the plant is under threat of extinction. However, it has been widely used in breeding programmes and is the ancestor of many of the white-flowered hybrids found in collections today.

The flowers, which are up to 12cm (5in) across when fully open, are held upright on the stems in a most appealing manner. They give off a sweet lilac scent. The sepals and petals, both a sparkling ivory white (sometimes showing a pink tinge), are narrow and gently recurving.

The trumpet-like lip is stained yellow within. Cymbidium eburneum is a parent of many of the modern hybrids – crossing with C. insigne produced C. Gottianum. A cool period from summer through autumn is necessary to initiate flower formation.

QUICK REFERENCE

PLANT SIZE
Up to 50cm (20in), sometimes more.

NUMBER OF FLOWERS
1–3 per stem.

FLOWERING PERIOD
Winter to spring.

REGULARITY OF FLOWERING
Annually.

HABIT OF GROWTH
Evergreen sympodial orchid that has very small pseudobulbs.

BEST WAY TO GROW
Grow in a container that restricts the roots and is filled with epiphytic orchid compost, preferably with added rockwool.

GENERAL CARE
Cool growing (min 10-13ºC/50-55ºF; max 21-24ºC/ 70-75ºF). Shade from direct sun in summer; full light in winter. Water freely when in full growth and mist daily; water less in winter. Feed every 3 to 4 weeks when growing strongly in spring and summer.

PROPAGATION
Divide a congested plant after flowering; pot up dormant pseudobulbs separately.

EASE OF CULTIVATION
Some experience required.

Cymbidium Gleneagles 'Cooksbridge Delight'

The grex Gleneagles was bred from Cymbidium Putana and C. Precious Pink and was registered in 1985. It originated from McBean's Orchids, a nursery that specialises in cymbidiums and which has produced many fine hybrids. Gleneagles is classified as an intermediate. 'Cooksbridge Delight' is a selected form, others including 'Cooksbridge Advent'.

The flowers, which are up to 10cm (4in) across, are an appealing fresh cherry-blossom pink, with darker streaking on the petals and sepals. The lips are liberally spotted with a richer pink and have yellow bases. A cool period from summer through autumn is necessary to initiate flower formation.

QUICK REFERENCE

PLANT SIZE
Up to 45cm (18in) when in flower.

NUMBER OF FLOWERS
Up to 12 or more per stem.

FLOWERING PERIOD
Usually mid-winter, though earlier or later flowering is also possible.

REGULARITY OF FLOWERING
Usually annually, but can be reluctant without a cool period during late summer–autumn.

HABIT OF GROWTH
Evergreen sympodial orchid that has pseudobulbs.

BEST WAY TO GROW
Grow in a container that restricts the roots and is filled with epiphytic orchid compost, preferably with added rockwool.

GENERAL CARE
Cool growing (min 10-13ºC/50-55ºF; max 21-24ºC/ 70-75ºF). Shade from direct sun in summer; full light in winter. Water freely when in full growth and mist daily; water less in winter. Feed every 3 to 4 weeks when growing strongly in spring and summer.

PROPAGATION
Divide a congested plant after flowering; pot up dormant pseudobulbs separately.

EASE OF CULTIVATION
An easy orchid for beginners, though not always easy to bring into flower.

Cymbidium Kings Loch 'Cooksbridge'

Kings Loch was bred from Cymbidium King Arthur and C. Loch Lomond, registration taking place in 1985. It was produced at McBean's Orchids, the originator of many fine cymbidiums. 'Cooksbridge', classified as a miniature cymbidium, is one of a number of selected forms.

A particular feature of the grex is the wide spacing of the flowers on the flower stem, and the way they appear to point in all directions – this allows individuals to be examined in detail. Around 8cm (3in) across, the flowers are a waxy yellowish green and the lips are marked with dark red. For a clearer base colour, look for the selected form 'Miniature Yellow'. This cymbidium benefits particularly from firm potting, so the use of terrestrial orchid compost is recommended. A cool period from summer through autumn is necessary to initiate flower formation.

QUICK REFERENCE

PLANT SIZE
Up to 45cm (18in) when in flower.

NUMBER OF FLOWERS
Up to 12 or more per stem.

FLOWERING PERIOD
Usually mid- to late winter, though flowers can also be produced just before or after.

REGULARITY OF FLOWERING
Usually annually, but can be reluctant without a cool period during late summer–autumn.

HABIT OF GROWTH
Evergreen sympodial orchid that has pseudobulbs.

BEST WAY TO GROW
Grow in a container that restricts the roots and is filled with terrestrial orchid compost, preferably with added rockwool.

GENERAL CARE
Cool growing (min 10-13ºC/50-55ºF; max 21-24ºC/ 70-75ºF). Shade from direct sun in summer; full light in winter. Water freely when in full growth and mist daily; water less in winter. Feed every 3 to 4 weeks when growing strongly in spring and summer.

PROPAGATION
Divide a congested plant after flowering; pot up dormant pseudobulbs separately.

EASE OF CULTIVATION
An easy orchid for beginners, though not always easy to bring into flower.

Cymbidium Ming 'Pagoda'

This is a rare hybrid, but a fairly tried and tested one. The grex was registered in 1969 by Rod McLellan Co., the result of crossing Cymbidium Oiso with C. Rusper. It is an intermediate cymbidium. There are a number of selected forms in commerce, others including 'Manchu'.

The flowers are small, at about 6cm (2½in) across, but produced in quantity on stems that arch over under their weight. They are greenish gold and waxy in texture, with relatively narrow petals and sepals. The lips, a pale ivory-cream, are strongly edged and spotted with maroon. A cool period from summer through autumn is necessary in order to initiate flower formation.

QUICK REFERENCE

PLANT SIZE
Up to 60cm (24in) when in flower.

NUMBER OF FLOWERS
Up to 20 or more per stem.

FLOWERING PERIOD
Autumn and late winter, sometimes spring.

REGULARITY OF FLOWERING
Usually annually, but can be reluctant without a cool period during late summer-autumn.

HABIT OF GROWTH
Evergreen sympodial orchid that has pseudobulbs.

BEST WAY TO GROW
Grow in a container that restricts the roots and is filled with epiphytic orchid compost, preferably with added rockwool.

GENERAL CARE
Cool growing (min 10-13ºC/50-55ºF; max 21-24ºC/ 70-75ºF). Shade from direct sun in summer; full light in winter. Water freely when in full growth and mist daily; water less in winter. Feed every 3 to 4 weeks when growing strongly in spring and summer.

PROPAGATION
Divide a congested plant after flowering; pot up dormant pseudobulbs separately.

EASE OF CULTIVATION
An easy orchid for beginners, though not always easy to bring into flower.

Cymbidium Peachlet

Peachlet was registered in 1989 by Geyserland, the progeny of a cross between Cymbidium Pink Peach and C. Ringlet. It is classified as an intermediate cymbidium, meaning the plant is of average size. It has been used in breeding to produce further pink-flowered hybrids.

The flowers, which are up to 10cm (4in) across, are a delightful clear pink with warmer shadings. The flaring, trumpet-like lips are edged with a warmer pink and spotted with deep pink and yellow towards the base.

The pink spots merge towards the edge. Keeping the plant cool during late summer and through autumn helps initiate flower production.

QUICK REFERENCE

PLANT SIZE
Up to 60cm (24in).

NUMBER OF FLOWERS
Up to 10 per stem.

FLOWERING PERIOD
Autumn and late winter, sometimes spring.

REGULARITY OF FLOWERING
Usually annually, but can be reluctant without a cool period during late summer–autumn.

HABIT OF GROWTH
Evergreen sympodial orchid that has pseudobulbs.

BEST WAY TO GROW
Grow in a container that restricts the roots and is filled with epiphytic orchid compost, preferably with added rockwool.

GENERAL CARE
Cool growing (min 10-13ºC/50-55ºF; max 21-24ºC/ 70-75ºF). Shade from direct sun in summer; full light in winter. Water freely when in full growth and mist daily; water less in winter. Feed every 3 to 4 weeks when growing strongly in spring and summer.

PROPAGATION
Divide a congested plant after flowering; pot up dormant pseudobulbs separately.

EASE OF CULTIVATION
An easy orchid for beginners, though not always easy to bring into flower.

Cymbidium Plemont

Plemont is a fairly recent introduction, having been bred from Cymbidium Beresford and C. Highland Advent. It was registered in 1996 and is classified as a miniature.

The flowers are perhaps among the most flamboyant of any of the breed, boldly flaring open to 10cm (4in) across or more. They have the greenish cast - and waxy texture - that typifies so many cymbidiums. Both petals and sepals are streaked darker.

The lips are dramatically edged and flecked with a contrasting maroon. A cool period from summer through autumn is necessary to initiate flower formation.

QUICK REFERENCE

PLANT SIZE
Up to 60cm (24in).

NUMBER OF FLOWERS
Up to 10 or more per stem.

FLOWERING PERIOD
Autumn and late winter, sometimes into spring.

REGULARITY OF FLOWERING
Usually annually, but can be reluctant without a cool period during late summer-autumn.

HABIT OF GROWTH
Evergreen sympodial orchid that has pseudobulbs.

BEST WAY TO GROW
Grow in a container that restricts the roots and is filled with epiphytic orchid compost, preferably with added rockwool.

GENERAL CARE
Cool growing (min 10-13°C/50-55°F; max 21-24°C/ 70-75°F). Shade from direct sun in summer; full light in winter. Water freely when in full growth and mist daily; water less in winter. Feed every 3 to 4 weeks when growing strongly in spring and summer.

PROPAGATION
Divide a congested plant after flowering; pot up dormant pseudobulbs separately.

EASE OF CULTIVATION
An easy orchid for beginners, though not always easy to bring into flower.

Cymbidium Red Baker

Red Baker was registered in 1993. Its name is a clever conflation of those of its parents – Cymbidium Red Beauty and C. Doctor Baker.
This plant is classified as an intermediate cymbidium.

Red orchids are always exciting and this is no exception, though the red is closer to a deep dusky pink than a true clear red. The flowers are produced in quantity over a six- to eight-week period. Opening to 8cm (3in) across, the petals and sepals are a warm, glowing pinkish red.

The lips are darker, and are heavily marked with yellow. A well-grown specimen in full flower makes an impressive plant. A cool period from summer through autumn is necessary to initiate flower formation.

QUICK REFERENCE

PLANT SIZE
Up to 50cm (20in) when in flower.

NUMBER OF FLOWERS
Up to 20 or more flowers per stem.

FLOWERING PERIOD
Late summer to autumn.

REGULARITY OF FLOWERING
Usually annually, but can be reluctant without a cool period during late summer–autumn.

HABIT OF GROWTH
Evergreen sympodial orchid that has pseudobulbs.

BEST WAY TO GROW
Grow in a container that restricts the roots and is filled with epiphytic orchid compost, preferably with added rockwool.

GENERAL CARE
Cool growing (min 10-13ºC/50-55ºF; max 21-24ºC/ 70-75ºF). Shade from direct sun in summer; full light in winter. Water freely when in full growth and mist daily; water less in winter. Feed every 3 to 4 weeks when growing strongly in spring and summer.

PROPAGATION
Divide a congested plant after flowering; pot up dormant pseudobulbs separately.

EASE OF CULTIVATION
An easy orchid for beginners, though not always easy to bring into flower.

Cymbidium Summer Pearl 'Senne'

The grex Summer Pearl was registered in 1984 by the breeder Geyserland. Its parents are Cymbidium Peter Pan and C. Trigo Royale. It is classified as a miniature or compact type, so takes up rather less space than some other hybrids. As a result it has been much used in breeding programmes to create further plants of relatively modest size. Selected forms come in a range of colours.

'Senne' is a form with fragrant, greenish yellow, waxy-textured flowers that are around 5cm (2in) across when fully open. The lips are heavily spotted with maroon. Initially pendent, the flowers turn upright as they open.

The plant will stay in flower for six to eight weeks. 'Sonia' is a pink form.
A cool period from summer through autumn is necessary to initiate flower formation.

QUICK REFERENCE

PLANT SIZE
Up to 60cm (24in).

NUMBER OF FLOWERS
Up to 10 or more per stem.

FLOWERING PERIOD
Late summer to autumn, sometimes later.

REGULARITY OF FLOWERING
Usually annually, but can be reluctant without a cool period during late summer–autumn.

HABIT OF GROWTH
Evergreen sympodial orchid that has pseudobulbs.

BEST WAY TO GROW
Grow in a container that restricts the roots and is filled with epiphytic orchid compost, preferably with added rockwool.

GENERAL CARE
Cool growing (min 10-13ºC/50-55ºF; max 21-24ºC/ 70-75ºF). Shade from direct sun in summer; full light in winter. Water freely when in full growth and mist daily; water less in winter. Feed every 3 to 4 weeks when growing strongly in spring and summer.

PROPAGATION
Divide a congested plant after flowering; pot up dormant pseudobulbs separately.

EASE OF CULTIVATION
An easy orchid for beginners, though not always easy to bring into flower.

dendrobiums

With over 1,000 species - and new ones still being discovered - Dendrobium is one of the largest orchid genera, spread over a range that covers much of Asia down to Australia and parts of New Zealand. All dendrobiums have slender pseudobulbs that look like bamboo canes. However such is their diversity that generalisation over their care can be tricky, although most hybrids can be divided into one of two groups. Those with the Himalayan D. nobile in their parentage are cool growing and appreciate a dormant period in winter, when water can be withheld and they can lose all or most of their leaves. The Antipodean D. biggibum (syn. D. phalaenopsis) has spawned a vast tribe of plants, often referred to as phalaenopsis-type dendrobiums, and these like it slightly warmer. Extensive breeding within both groups has resulted in plants showing a wide colour range.

Dendrobium Delicatum

This is a primary hybrid, occurring naturally in rainforest areas of Australia, of the native Dendrobium kingianum and D. speciosum – both of which appear in some orchid catalogues. It is sometimes, erroneously, known as D. kingianum var. album. This is a popular orchid in Australia, where it is commonly used for breeding. Mature plants produce masses of flowers that are suitable for cutting.

The flowers, which are around 6cm (21/2in) across, sweetly fragrant and of pure glistening white, are produced in a profusion of sprays on the tips of canes. The lips are only very lightly marked with purple-pink. The flower spikes also last well, either on the plant or as cut flowers.

Even a small plant can fill a house with scent. The plant combines well with cattleyas and cymbidiums in an orchid collection. 'Apple Blossom' is a selection with pale pink flowers, while 'Pretty Good' is a luminous violet.

QUICK REFERENCE

PLANT SIZE
Up to 60cm (24in) when in flower.

NUMBER OF FLOWERS
Up to 20 flowers or more per cluster.

FLOWERING PERIOD
Late winter to early spring.

REGULARITY OF FLOWERING
Annually.

HABIT OF GROWTH
Evergreen sympodial orchid that has stem-like pseudobulbs.

BEST WAY TO GROW
Possibly best mounted on a bark slab, but can also be grown in a pot (preferably one that restricts the roots) containing coarse epiphytic orchid compost.

GENERAL CARE
Cool growing (min 10-13ºC/50-55ºF; max 21-24ºC/ 70-75ºF). Shade in summer; full light in winter. Mist daily when in active growth, water freely (but keep dry in winter) and apply fertiliser every 3 to 4 weeks during the period after flowering.

PROPAGATION
Take cuttings of leafless stems or remove any keikis that appear.

EASE OF CULTIVATION
Some experience required.

Dendrobium Lloyd Stainton

This grex has two species as its immediate parents, Dendrobium superbiens and D. canaliculatum, from New Guinea and northeast Australia – demonstrating that wild plants still have a significant part to play in the development of new orchids. It was registered in 1986 by Lonne's Nursery, an Australian breeder of orchids.

The plant produces sprays of bluish purple, delicately veined flowers, up to 5cm (2in) across, on tall, erect stems that rise proudly above the strappy, rich green leaves.

The delicate sepals can twist at the back of the flower, while the petals flare backwards to show off the more richly coloured lips.

QUICK REFERENCE

PLANT SIZE
Up to 60cm (24in) when in flower.

NUMBER OF FLOWERS
Up to 20 or more per stem.

FLOWERING PERIOD
Late winter to early spring.

REGULARITY OF FLOWERING
Annually.

HABIT OF GROWTH
Evergreen sympodial orchid with elongated, stem-like pseudobulbs.

BEST WAY TO GROW
Grow in a pot that restricts the roots, and which contains epiphytic orchid compost. (The plant can be up to 10 times as tall as the pot is wide.) Alternatively, tie to a piece of bark.

GENERAL CARE
Intermediate growing (min 14-19ºC/57-66ºF; max 30-33ºC/86-91ºF). Light shade in summer; full light from autumn to spring. Water freely when in active growth and mist daily; reduce watering in winter. Feed every 3 to 4 weeks during the period after flowering.

PROPAGATION
Divide a congested plant in spring or take stem cuttings of older, leafless stems. Detach any keikis that form.

EASE OF CULTIVATION
Some experience required.

Dendrobium nobile

Dendrobium nobile is possibly the granddaddy of them all. Certainly, its significance in breeding programmes can hardly be overstated, and a vast number of hybrids can trace their ancestry back to it. Dendrobium nobile itself hails from the Himalaya, south China and Taiwan, where it naturally grows epiphytically.

This orchid makes a tall, elegant plant that out of flower could almost pass as a miniature bamboo.

The attractive violet-pink flowers, which are up to 8cm (3in) across, hang down in a most appealing way. They are carried in pairs on short stems along the cane-like stems and look as though they have been brushed with a darker purple. The lips are dramatically marked with white and a rich dark purple. Whatever the claims of its hybrids, the original parent still deserves a place in the collections of dedicated enthusiasts.

QUICK REFERENCE

PLANT SIZE
Up to 45cm (18in).

NUMBER OF FLOWERS
Up to 8 or more per stem.

FLOWERING PERIOD
Winter to early spring.

REGULARITY OF FLOWERING
Annually.

HABIT OF GROWTH
Semi-evergreen sympodial orchid with elongated, stem-like pseudobulbs.

BEST WAY TO GROW
Grow in a pot that restricts the roots, and which contains coarse epiphytic orchid compost. (The plant can be up to 10 times as tall as the pot is wide.) Alternatively, tie to a piece of bark.

GENERAL CARE
Cool growing (min 10-13ºC/50-55ºF; max 21-24ºC/ 70-75ºF), although it is tolerant of higher temperatures. Light shade in summer; full light from autumn to spring. Water freely when in active growth and mist daily; reduce watering in winter. Add fertiliser every 3 to 4 weeks during the period after flowering.

PROPAGATION
Divide a congested plant in spring or take stem cuttings of older, leafless stems. Detach any keikis that form.

EASE OF CULTIVATION
Some experience required.

Dendrobium Prima Donna

This hybrid was created at the Yamamoto Nursery and was registered in 1979. Its parents are Dendrobium Milky Way and D. Bright Star.

Prima donnas are accustomed to being the centre of attention, and this plant usually is when the flowers emerge. They are almost as flamboyant as those of some of the cattleyas and are so clustered on the stems that they almost obscure the leaves.

Reaching up to 8cm (3in) across, they are among the largest you are likely to find on a dendrobium. Petals and sepals are white, brushed with pink, while the lips have the usual yellow markings towards the centre. All flower parts are appealingly crimped at the edges.

QUICK REFERENCE

PLANT SIZE
Up to 45cm (18in).

NUMBER OF FLOWERS
Up to 10-12 per stem or more.

FLOWERING PERIOD
Late winter to spring.

REGULARITY OF FLOWERING
Annually.

HABIT OF GROWTH
Semi-evergreen sympodial orchid with elongated, cane-like pseudobulbs.

BEST WAY TO GROW
Grow in a small pot of very open, epiphytic orchid compost.

GENERAL CARE
Cool growing (min 10-13°C/50-55°F; max 21-24°C/ 70-75°F). Light shade in summer; full light from autumn to spring. Water freely when in active growth and mist daily; reduce watering in winter. Add fertiliser every 3 to 4 weeks during the period after flowering.

PROPAGATION
Divide a congested plant in spring or take stem cuttings of older, leafless stems. Detach keikis as and when they form.

EASE OF CULTIVATION
Some experience required.

Dendrobium Stardust 'Chyomi'

Stardust's parents are the species Dendrobium unicum, found in Laos and Thailand, and D. Ukon. This plant was registered in 1986. 'Fire Bird' is a similar selection to 'Chyomi', but is more richly coloured.

The soft apricot-orange flowers, which are around 6cm (21/2in) across, are of considerable distinction. They are produced on short stems from the main canes, appearing to cluster among the leaves. Petals and sepals show a uniform, virtually unmarked, even colour, while the lips are delicately veined with red. The sepals are narrower than the petals, which re-curve gently at the edges. Established plants can be in flower for up to four months. The flowers turn a richer colour as they age on the plant.

QUICK REFERENCE

PLANT SIZE
Up to 50cm (20in).

NUMBER OF FLOWERS
Up to 20 flowers or more per stem.

FLOWERING PERIOD
Mid-winter to spring.

REGULARITY OF FLOWERING
An established plant should flower every year.

HABIT OF GROWTH
Semi-evergreen sympodial orchid with elongated, stem-like pseudobulbs.

BEST WAY TO GROW
Grow in a pot that restricts the roots, and which contains coarse epiphytic orchid compost. (The plant can be up to 10 times as tall as the pot is wide.)

GENERAL CARE
Cool growing (min 10-13°C/50-55°F; max 21-24°C/ 70-75°F). Light shade in summer; full light from autumn to spring. Water freely when in active growth and mist daily; reduce watering in winter. Add fertiliser every 3 to 4 weeks during the period after flowering.

PROPAGATION
Divide a congested plant in spring or take stem cuttings of older, leafless stems. Detach keikis as and when they form.

EASE OF CULTIVATION
Some experience required.

Dendrobium Thai Ruby

Thai Ruby was registered in 1992. Its parents are Dendrobium Thai Pearl and the species D. biggibum, which is a semi-evergreen epiphyte from Queensland, Australia. The species is variable and a wide range of colourful hybrids, sometimes loosely referred to as phalaenopsis-type dendrobiums, has been bred from it. Deep Red Thai Beauty is a similar hybrid, but with dark red flowers.

A casual glance might persuade you this was a phalaenopsis though the flowers, which are around 8cm (3in) across, have somewhat more pointed sepals. The colour is a rich fuchsia pink, the lips being a warmer purple.

The flowers are carried in great style on slender stems that are upright initially but arch over as the upper flowers open again like a phalaenopsis. The stems are splendid for cutting.

QUICK REFERENCE

PLANT SIZE
Up to 60cm (24in) when in flower.

NUMBER OF FLOWERS
Up to 10 flowers or more per stem.

FLOWERING PERIOD
Late winter to spring.

REGULARITY OF FLOWERING
Annually.

HABIT OF GROWTH
Evergreen sympodial orchid with elongated, stem-like pseudobulbs.

BEST WAY TO GROW
Grow in a pot that restricts the roots, and which contains epiphytic orchid compost. (The plant can be up to 10 times as tall as the pot is wide.) Alternatively, tie to a piece of bark.

GENERAL CARE
Intermediate growing (min 14-19°C/57-66°F; max 30-33°C/86-91°F). Light shade in summer; full light from autumn to spring. Water freely when in active growth and mist daily; reduce watering in winter. Add fertiliser every 3 to 4 weeks during the growing period after flowering.

PROPAGATION
Divide a congested plant in spring or take stem cuttings of older, leafless stems.

EASE OF CULTIVATION
Some experience required.

Dendrobium Victorian King

This is a relatively new grex that was registered in 1999. Its parents are the variable species Dendrobium kingianum – found in New South Wales and Queensland, Australia – and the grex D. Zip.

The plant is a substantial one, with firm stems and broad, glossy green leaves. The flowers, when they appear, are something of a surprise, airily carried in loose clusters on slender stems that emerge from between the leaves. They are up to 4cm (11/2in) across with elegantly pointed, almost triangular purplish pink petals and sepals.

The lips are mottled with a darker colour. Victorian King has something of the style of its parent species, but makes a bigger, more robust plant a good contrast to other more highly bred dendrobiums.

QUICK REFERENCE

PLANT SIZE
Up to 30cm (12in) when in flower.

NUMBER OF FLOWERS
Up to 9 or more per cluster.

FLOWERING PERIOD
Winter to spring.

REGULARITY OF FLOWERING
Annually.

HABIT OF GROWTH
Evergreen sympodial orchid with narrowly conical pseudobulbs.

BEST WAY TO GROW
Grow in a pot that restricts the roots, and which contains coarse epiphytic orchid compost. (The plant can be up to 10 times as tall as the pot is wide.) Alternatively, tie to a piece of bark.

GENERAL CARE
Cool growing (min 10–13ºC/50–55ºF; max 21–24ºC/ 70–75ºF). Light shade in summer; full light from autumn to spring. Water freely when in active growth and mist daily; reduce watering in winter. Feed every 3 to 4 weeks during the growing period after flowering.

PROPAGATION
Divide a congested plant in spring or take stem cuttings of older, leafless stems. Detach any keikis that form.

EASE OF CULTIVATION
Some experience required.

Dendrobium White Pony

White Pony originates from the famous Yamamoto Nursery, where it was bred from Dendrobium Anglow and D. Red Star. The nursery specialises in dendrobiums and is the creator of many fine hybrids. Registered in 1975, White Pony has stood the test of time and has been used as the parent of several other hybrids of distinction.

The plant is robust and healthy, with thick, substantial canes and glossy leaves. The flowers, which open from ivory buds, are carried singly or in small clusters on short stems from the main canes, usually the upper portion. Up to 7cm (2¾in) across, the flowers are pure white with a pronounced red blotch towards the centre of the lip. They persist on the plant for several weeks.

QUICK REFERENCE

PLANT SIZE
Up to 60cm (24in).

NUMBER OF FLOWERS
Up to 9 flowers or more per stem, more on a larger, established plant.

FLOWERING PERIOD
Late winter to spring.

REGULARITY OF FLOWERING
Annually.

HABIT OF GROWTH
Evergreen sympodial orchid with elongated, stem-like pseudobulbs.

BEST WAY TO GROW
Grow in a pot or basket of epiphytic compost; alternatively, mount on bark.

GENERAL CARE
Intermediate growing (min 14–19ºC/57–66ºF; max 30–33ºC/86–91ºF). Light shade in summer; full light from autumn to spring. Water freely when in active growth and mist daily; reduce watering in winter. Feed every 3 to 4 weeks during the growing period after flowering.

PROPAGATION
Divide a congested plant in spring or take stem cuttings of older, leafless stems.

EASE OF CULTIVATION
Some experience required.

odontoglossums

The odontoglossums are a vast group that comprises not only Odontoglossum itself but a number of related genera and the many hybrids that have been produced from extensive interbreeding – these plants are promiscuous. In the wild, they are found growing mostly at high altitude in Central and South America, so the majority of the hybrids appreciate cool conditions. But breeding outside the group – with Brassia, for example – has produced plants that tolerate warmer temperatures and, viewed as a whole, the alliance shows greater diversity than any other group of orchids – with a comparably wide colour range.

Most odontoglossums grow and flower in a nine-month cycle, so plants can flower at different times each year. Growing a number of different examples of these plants, therefore, can create a collection that produces flowers almost throughout the year.

Beallara Tahoma Glacier 'Green'

This intergeneric hybrid has a complex parentage, involving Brassia x Cochlioda x Miltonia x Odontoglossum. It was created in 1970 from a cross between Miltassia Cartagena and Odontioda Alaskan Sunset.

The flowers of this plant are large, up to 13cm (5in) across, long lasting and well spaced on strong, upright spikes. The petals and sepals are a translucent off-white, beguilingly tinged centrally with ice green and more richly marked with deep reddish pink towards the base.

The edges of the lips are frilled and greenish, and have red and yellow marks towards the centre. This is a modest plant, but is of considerable distinction, and is seen at its best when the flowers are back-lit – for instance if it is grown on a windowsill. Then the flowers really sparkle.

QUICK REFERENCE

PLANT SIZE
Up to 75cm (30in).

NUMBER OF FLOWERS
Up to 9 or more per stem.

FLOWERING PERIOD
Flowers can be produced at almost any time of year.

REGULARITY OF FLOWERING
An established plant can be more or less permanently in flower.

HABIT OF GROWTH
Evergreen sympodial orchid that has green pseudobulbs.

BEST WAY TO GROW
Grow in a pot of epiphytic orchid compost.

GENERAL CARE
Cool growing (min 10-13ºC/50-55ºF; max 21-24ºC/ 70-75ºF). Shade from hot sun in summer; full light in winter. Water freely when in active growth and mist daily; reduce watering in winter. Feed every 3 to 4 weeks when in active growth.

PROPAGATION
Divide this particular plant only when absolutely necessary.

EASE OF CULTIVATION
An easy-to-grow hybrid.

Burrageara Nelly Isler

Burrageara is a complex cross, named in honour of the American orchid grower Albert Cameron Burrage, involving Cochlioda, Miltonia, Odontoglossum and Oncidium. The genus was established in 1927 but this hybrid is of much more recent origin, having been registered in 1995. Its parents are Burrageara Stefan Isler and Miltonia Kensington.

The bold red flowers of this plant are up to 6cm (21/2in) across and they open flat. The lips are orange with a red flare at the yellow centre. The orange breaks into pink towards the edge. Like other similar orchids belonging to the odontoglossum alliance, Nelly Isler has been bred to thrive in centrally heated living rooms. Be careful not to keep the plant too warm, however, as a high temperature can inhibit flowering.

The flowering stems are so sturdy that staking is not always strictly necessary.

QUICK REFERENCE

PLANT SIZE
Up to 60cm (24in) when in flower.

NUMBER OF FLOWERS
Up to 10 flowers or more per stem.

FLOWERING PERIOD
Nelly Isler can flower at virtually any time of year.

REGULARITY OF FLOWERING
With appropriate care, an established plant can be more or less continuously in bloom.

HABIT OF GROWTH
Compact, evergreen sympodial orchid with green pseudobulbs.

BEST WAY TO GROW
Grow in a small pot containing epiphytic orchid compost.

GENERAL CARE
Cool growing (min 10-13°C/50-55°F; max 21-24°C/ 70-75°F). Shade in summer; full light in winter. Water throughout the year and mist daily in spring and summer. Feed every 3 to 4 weeks in spring and summer, when growth is at its strongest.

PROPAGATION
Divide when the plant outgrows its pot, probably every 2 to 3 years.

EASE OF CULTIVATION
This is a very easy hybrid to grow, and as such is suitable for beginners.

Burrageara Stefan Isler

This intergeneric hybrid involves Cochlioda, Miltonia, Odontoglossum and Oncidium. Its parents are the complex cross Vuylstekeara Edna and the species Oncidium leucochilum, which is from Mexico, Honduras and Guatemala. Stefan Isler was registered in 1990.

The plant produces tall spikes of flowers with bright red petals and sepals and fiddle-like, beautifully marked lips - a distinctive trait that betrays the genes inherited from Miltonia. Basically pink, the lips are richly blotched with orange red - some of the blotches being edged with yellow. Oncidium has influenced the plant's size as it is much more compact than some other hybrids - though no less robust - making it an ideal choice if you have only limited space but are looking for a truly eye-catching specimen. This is a vibrant orchid that fully deserves its popularity.

QUICK REFERENCE

PLANT SIZE
Up to 60cm (24in) when in flower.

NUMBER OF FLOWERS
Up to 10 flowers or more per stem.

FLOWERING PERIOD
Virtually any time of year.

REGULARITY OF FLOWERING
When mature, the plant will flower several times during the year.

HABIT OF GROWTH
Evergreen sympodial orchid that has green pseudobulbs.

BEST WAY TO GROW
Grow in a container that restricts the roots and is filled with fine-grade epiphytic orchid compost.

GENERAL CARE
Cool growing (min 10-13°C/50-55°F; max 21-24°C/ 70-75°F). Shade in summer; full light in winter. Water throughout the year and mist daily in spring and summer. Feed every 3 to 4 weeks in spring and summer, when growth is at its strongest.

PROPAGATION
Divide when the plant outgrows its pot, probably every 2 to 3 years.

EASE OF CULTIVATION
This is a very easy hybrid to grow, and as such it is suitable for beginners.

Colmanara Wildcat 'Cheetah'

Colmanaras are trigeneric hybrids of Miltonia, Oncidium and Odontoglossum. Sir Jeremiah Colman, in whose honour they are named, was a prominent British orchid grower of the first half of the 20th century. Wildcat arose from a cross between Odontonia Rustic Bridge and Odontocidium Crowburgh, and was registered in 1992.

The plant looks like an oncidium, but has somewhat bigger flowers, up to 7cm (23⁄4in) across, that are maroon and yellow with mahogany bars and white lips. They look like butterflies that have alighted on the long, arching stems among the substantial, glossy green leaves, and can last for four to six weeks. The hybrid group also includes 'Jaguar', 'Ocelot' and 'Bobcat'. Like the other oncidiums, this hybrid has pseudobulbs. It tolerates lower light levels than some other odontoglossums – if the leaves show black spots, reduce the light.

QUICK REFERENCE

PLANT SIZE
Up to 90cm (36in) high when in flower.

NUMBER OF FLOWERS
A mature plant can produce 40 flowers per spike.

FLOWERING PERIOD
The plant can flower at virtually any time of year.

REGULARITY OF FLOWERING
With appropriate cultivation, the plant should flower 2 or 3 times a year.

HABIT OF GROWTH
Evergreen sympodial orchid that has pseudobulbs.

BEST WAY TO GROW
Grow in a container filled with epiphytic orchid compost.

GENERAL CARE
Cool growing (min 10-13ºC/50-55ºF; max 21-24ºC/ 70-75ºF) to intermediate growing (min 14-19ºC/ 57-66ºF; max 30-33ºC/ 86-91ºF). Shade in summer; full light in winter. Water freely when in active growth in spring and summer and mist daily. Water sparingly in winter. Feed every 3 to 4 weeks when in full growth.

PROPAGATION
Divide this plant when its roots fill the container.

EASE OF CULTIVATION
This is an easy orchid to grow and makes an excellent choice for anyone starting a collection.

Odontioda Gorey Castle

Gorey Castle was registered in 1986, the result of a cross between Odontoglossum Nicky Strauss and Odontioda Jumbo. Odontioda itself is a hybrid genus of Odontoglossum and Cochlioda. Gorey Castle is rare in collections.

The large, rounded flowers, which open flat to 8cm (3in) across, are clear sugar pink and generously blotched with a warm pinkish red. They are carried well above the leaves on upright to slightly arching stems. The edges of the petals and sepals are attractively ruffled, which is a feature of all odontiodas. Staking is essential, otherwise the weight of the flowers can cause the slender stems to break. In an odontioda collection, Gorey Castle would make a pleasing foil to the more richly coloured hybrids.

QUICK REFERENCE

PLANT SIZE
Up to 45cm (18in) when in flower.

NUMBER OF FLOWERS
Up to 7 or more flowers per stem.

FLOWERING PERIOD
Usually late winter to spring, although flowers can be produced at almost any time of year.

REGULARITY OF FLOWERING
An established plant will flower regularly.

HABIT OF GROWTH
Evergreen sympodial orchid with ovoid green pseudobulbs.

BEST WAY TO GROW
Grow in a pot filled with fine-grade epiphytic orchid compost, as the plant has fine roots.

GENERAL CARE
Cool growing (min 10-13°C/50-55°F; max 21-24°C/ 70-75°F). Shade from hot sun in summer; full light in winter. Water freely when in full growth and mist daily. Reduce watering in winter. Feed every 3 to 4 weeks when in active growth.

PROPAGATION
Divide when the plant becomes congested and its roots fill the container.

EASE OF CULTIVATION
Odontiodas are easy orchids for beginners.

Odontoglossum Violetta von Holm

There are many odontoglossum hybrids, all highly variable. Violetta von Holm, registered in 1994, arose as a result of crossing two Central American species, Odontoglossum bictoniense and O. rossii (as they were then called). They are now usually classified within Lemboglossum.

This hybrid has strong patterning on the flowers. When fully open, they are around 4cm (11/2in) across. The sepals and upper petals are strongly barred with dark mahogany red over a base colour of crocus yellow, and the lips are a vibrant, bright pinkish mauve. Each flower stem is tall and upright and carries several panicles of flowers. This compact hybrid, like most odontoglossums, is suitable for growing on a windowsill. A mature, well-grown specimen in full flower is an impressive thing, bearing up to 50 flowers at once.

QUICK REFERENCE

PLANT SIZE
Up to 60cm (24in) when in flower.

NUMBER OF FLOWERS
Usually up to 10 or more flowers per spike.

FLOWERING PERIOD
Usually autumn, but flowers can also be produced at other times of year.

REGULARITY OF FLOWERING
An established plant can flower twice a year.

HABIT OF GROWTH
Evergreen sympodial orchid that has ovoid pseudobulbs.

BEST WAY TO GROW
Grow in a pot that constricts the roots. Use a fine-grade epiphytic compost.

GENERAL CARE
Cool growing (min 10-13ºC/50-55ºF; max 21-24ºC/ 70-75ºF). Shade from hot sun in summer; full light in winter. Water freely when in active growth and mist daily - in summer, the compost should be allowed to dry out slightly between waterings; reduce watering in winter. Feed every 3 to 4 weeks when in active growth.

PROPAGATION
Divide the plant only when it seems absolutely necessary.

EASE OF CULTIVATION
This is an easy orchid to grow.

Odontonia Boussole 'Blanche'

This hybrid was developed in France. The grex Boussole is of some age, having been registered in 1942 as a cross between Miltonia Princess Mary and Odontoglossum Nabab. Odontonias are hybrids of Odontoglossum and Miltoniopsis, the flowers of most showing more allegiance to the latter. The opposite is the case here, however, and the presence of Odontoglossum crispum – which has produced all the modern white hybrids – in its lineage is clear.

The unopened buds are pink, but show a much paler pink on opening, albeit with a pronounced tinge of that colour on the inside of the sepals. The centres of the flowers, which open to 8cm (3in) across and can persist for several weeks, are patterned lightly with uneven brownish red speckles.

QUICK REFERENCE

PLANT SIZE
Up to 30cm (12in) when in flower.

NUMBER OF FLOWERS
Up to 5 flowers or more per stem.

FLOWERING PERIOD
Usually winter, though flowers can also be produced at other times of year.

REGULARITY OF FLOWERING
An established plant can be more or less permanently in flower.

HABIT OF GROWTH
Evergreen sympodial orchid that has green pseudobulbs.

BEST WAY TO GROW
Grow in a pot of fine-grade epiphytic orchid compost, as the plant has a fine root system.

GENERAL CARE
Cool growing (min 10-13°C/50-55°F; max 21-24°C/ 70-75°F). Shade from hot sun in summer; full light in winter. Water freely when in full growth and mist daily. Water sparingly in winter. Feed every 3 to 4 weeks when in active growth.

PROPAGATION
Divide only when absolutely necessary.

EASE OF CULTIVATION
An easy orchid for a beginner.

Oncidium Ornithocurvum

Ornithocurvum is a hybrid of two species, Oncidium ornithorhynchum, a species with dainty flowers that occurs in south Mexico, Guatemala, El Salvador and Costa Rica, and O. incurvum, an elegant species from Mexico with fragrant white and pink flowers. This hybrid was registered in 1961.

The lacy, rich pink flowers are 2.5cm (1in) across and are carried in quantity and in elegant style on long, arching stems. Flower colour in itself distinguishes the plant, as most other oncidiums have yellow flowers. The flowers are fragrant too, making this a highly desirable plant. They contrast well with the broad, bright green leaves. Even if the individual flowers are not striking on their own, a mature plant in full flower is quite a sight. The plant benefits from a brief rest after flowering.

QUICK REFERENCE

PLANT SIZE
Up to 60cm (24in) or more.

NUMBER OF FLOWERS
Upwards of 12 per stem.

FLOWERING PERIOD
Autumn, at the end of the growing period.

REGULARITY OF FLOWERING
An established plant will flower annually.

HABIT OF GROWTH
Evergreen sympodial orchid with roughly oval or elongated pseudobulbs.

BEST WAY TO GROW
Grow in a pots of epiphytic compost, in a slatted basket or tied to a piece of bark.

GENERAL CARE
Cool growing (min 10-13°C/50-55°F; max 21-24°C/ 70-75°F). Shade from direct sun in summer; full light in winter. Water freely and mist daily when in active growth. Keep dry in winter. Feed every 3 to 4 weeks when in active growth.

PROPAGATION
Divide once congested. Pot up dormant pseudobulbs separately.

EASE OF CULTIVATION
Some experience required.

Oncidium Star Wars

Star Wars, commemorating the famous film of the same name, was registered in 1977. It was bred by Richard and Stella Mizuta, noted breeders of hybrids within the Oncidium/Miltonia alliance. Its parents are Oncidium Varimyre and O. Nonamyre. This tried and tested orchid has been used in breeding programmes to create further excellent plants.

The flowers, which are a mere 4cm (11/2in) across but produced in quantity, are carried in branching racemes on tall stems well above the glossy green leaves. They are predominantly yellow, the sepals and petals being banded with bright chestnut brown. The yellow lips are large, broad and flaring. At the centre of each is a ragged-edged bright brownish-red blotch. Staking is especially important to avoid the stems snapping under the weight of the flowers.

QUICK REFERENCE

PLANT SIZE
Up to 60cm (24in).

NUMBER OF FLOWERS
Up to 20-30 (or more) per stem.

FLOWERING PERIOD
Various periods during the year.

REGULARITY OF FLOWERING
The plant will flower twice or more a year as it matures.

HABIT OF GROWTH
Evergreen sympodial orchid that has pseudobulbs.

BEST WAY TO GROW
Grow in a pot or basket filled with epiphytic orchid compost.

GENERAL CARE
Cool growing (min 10-13ºC/50-55ºF; max 21-24ºC/ 70-75ºF) to intermediate growing (min 14-19ºC/ 57-66ºF; max 30-33ºC/ 86-91ºF). Shade during summer; full light in winter. Mist daily and water frequently when in active growth. Keep dry in winter. Feed every 3 to 4 weeks when in active growth.

PROPAGATION
Divide when the plant becomes congested.

EASE OF CULTIVATION
An easy hybrid that is suitable for beginners to grow.

Wilsonara Stirling Tiger

Wilsonaras are the result of a complex trigeneric cross of Cochlioda, Odontoglossum and Oncidium, named in honour of their original breeder. The parents of this particular plant are Odontioda Stirling and Odontocidium Tiger Hambühren. It was registered in 1999 by Mukoyama Orchids of Japan.

There are usually around seven flowers per stem, each one about 7cm (23/4in) across. (The stems themselves are up to 50cm (20in) in length.) A yellow-gold background is overlaid with blotches, and the petals and sepals are edged with a warm apricot red – that colour is especially seen at the petal tips.

The lips are prominent, delicately frilled and are a warm creamy yellow, delicately marked with maroon at the edges. Without doubt this is a great orchid.

QUICK REFERENCE

PLANT SIZE
Up to 60cm (24in) when in flower.

NUMBER OF FLOWERS
Up to 7 or more per stem.

FLOWERING PERIOD
Flowers can be produced at any time of year.

REGULARITY OF FLOWERING
An established plant can be more or less permanently in flower.

HABIT OF GROWTH
Evergreen, rhizomatous sympodial orchid with conical, flattened pseudobulbs.

BEST WAY TO GROW
Grow in a pot that restricts the roots. Use epiphytic orchid compost.

GENERAL CARE
Cool growing (min 10-13ºC/50-55ºF; max 21-24ºC/ 70-75ºF). Shade in summer; full light in winter. Water year-round, but less in winter. Do not mist. Feed every 3 to 4 weeks when in active growth.

PROPAGATION
Divide the plant when it becomes congested and its roots fill the container.

EASE OF CULTIVATION
An easy hybrid to grow.

slipper orchids

Orchids with flowers that have inflated lips – to trap pollinating insects – are loosely referred to as slipper orchids. Geographically, Cypripedium – scattered over the top of the globe, virtually hardy but tricky to grow so excluded here – forms the link between the Asian Paphiopedilum and the South American Phragmipedium. In the wild, all are considered endangered species.

Paphiopedilums are the most popular of the slipper orchids, and many have attractively marked leaves. Flower buds appear once the annual growth cycle is complete, and can be produced in succession. Phragmipediums, of which there is a smaller number, also bloom sequentially, and it is possible for a single spike to flower for as long as 18 months to two years.

Paphiopedilum Dellaina

Crossing Paphiopedilum delenatii, which is found in central Vietnam, with the Sumatran P. chamberlainianum (syn. P. victoria-reginae) produced this very popular primary hybrid in 1977. Back-crossing with P. chamberlainianum has resulted in plants that produce flowers of a more definite pink.

This plant produces its glistening white flowers, which are up to 10cm (4in) across, in succession over a long period when many other orchids are dormant. The basic colour is white, but the dorsal petal is delicately tinged with green and the pouch is pink. It is possible to find forms with a more pinkish coloration. Side petals show the slight bristling that is a characteristic of the genus. This hybrid has inherited its mottled leaves from P. delenatii. To maintain flower production, remove older flowers as they fade. In winter – when the plant may well be blooming – it is important to make sure the compost does not dry out between waterings.

QUICK REFERENCE

PLANT SIZE
Up to 30cm (12in).

NUMBER OF FLOWERS
2 or 3 flowers per stem.

FLOWERING PERIOD
Spring, though flowers can also be produced at other times of year.

REGULARITY OF FLOWERING
Intermittent.

HABIT OF GROWTH
Evergreen sympodial orchid that does not have pseudobulbs.

BEST WAY TO GROW
Grow in a pot that restricts the roots and which contains terrestrial orchid compost.

GENERAL CARE
Intermediate growing (min 14-19ºC/57-66ºF; max 30-33ºC/86-91ºF). Shade from hot sun in summer; full light in winter. Water freely when in active growth, more sparingly in winter but do not allow the compost to dry out between waterings. Do not mist. Feed every 3 to 4 weeks when growth is strong in spring and summer.

PROPAGATION
Generally not suitable for division, although large plants can be divided with care when repotting.

EASE OF CULTIVATION
This plant needs some care to ensure even flower production.

Paphiopedilum Helvetia

This plant is a primary hybrid of Paphiopedilum chamberlainianum (syn. P. victoria-reginae), from Sumatra, and the Filipino P. philippinense. It was registered in 1899 by the breeder D. Froebel. The grex name is the Latin name for Switzerland. This plant has definitely stood the test of time.

The flowers, which are up to 10cm (4in) across and carried on arching stems, have twisting green petals that are spotted and stained with purple. The pouches are green and white, while the green dorsal sepals are clearly lined darker. The plant's philippinense genes enable it to produce several flowers at once, and they will persist on the plant for several weeks. This is a compact plant – if you can't find Helvetia, try the roughly similar Honey (though, despite that name, neither has any fragrance).

QUICK REFERENCE

PLANT SIZE
Up to 40cm (16in) when in flower.

NUMBER OF FLOWERS
1-5 or more per stem.

FLOWERING PERIOD
Spring and summer.

REGULARITY OF FLOWERING
An established plant will flower regularly every year.

HABIT OF GROWTH
Evergreen sympodial orchid that does not have pseudobulbs.

BEST WAY TO GROW
Grow in terrestrial orchid compost with added bark chips to improve drainage, in a container that restricts the roots.

GENERAL CARE
Intermediate growing (min 14-19ºC/57-66ºF; max 30-33ºC/86-91ºF). In summer, shade from hot sun; full light in winter. Water freely when in full growth, sparingly in winter. Do not mist. Feed every 3 to 4 weeks when growth is at its strongest during spring and summer.

PROPAGATION
Generally not suitable for division, although large plants can be divided with care when repotting.

EASE OF CULTIVATION
This is an excellent choice for anyone starting a slipper orchid collection.

Paphiopedilum Jersey Freckles

This is a complex hybrid involving Indian species such as P. insigne, P. villosum and P. barbatum. Though its ancestry involves both cool- and intermediate-growing orchids, it prefers a warm position to a cool one. Its immediate parents are Paphiopedilum Saint Catherine's and P. Sparsholt, and it was registered in 1989.

The flowers, which are around 7cm (2¾in) across, are basically greenish yellow. The dorsal sepal, which is edged with white, is strongly marked with maroon-red blotches. Blotching also appears on the petals, but is more diffuse. The pouch is also blotched with dark red and has many hairs on the inside. Flowers appear singly, in winter, but can last a long time – over a period of around eight weeks. It is usual for a plant to bear just one flower, but larger, mature specimens can produce several.

QUICK REFERENCE

PLANT SIZE
Up to 30cm (12in) when in flower.

NUMBER OF FLOWERS
1 per stem.

FLOWERING PERIOD
Winter.

REGULARITY OF FLOWERING
Annually.

HABIT OF GROWTH
Evergreen sympodial orchid that does not have pseudobulbs.

BEST WAY TO GROW
Grow in a container that restricts the roots and is filled with epiphytic orchid compost with added bark chips.

GENERAL CARE
Intermediate growing (min 14-19ºC/57-66ºF; max 30-33ºC/86-91ºF). Shade from hot sun in summer; full light in winter. Water freely when in full growth, but do not mist. Water sparingly in winter. Feed every 3 to 4 weeks when growth is strongest during spring and summer.

PROPAGATION
Generally not suitable for division, although large plants can be divided with care when repotting.

EASE OF CULTIVATION
Some experience desirable.

Paphiopedilum Maudiae

Ease of cultivation has made this a popular orchid in collections ever since it was registered in 1900, and it makes a highly suitable beginner's plant for anyone new to the slipper orchids. Maudiae is a hybrid of two species: spring-flowering Paphiopedilum callosum - found in Thailand, Cambodia and south Vietnam - and P. lawrenceanum, which flowers in summer and is from Borneo.

The flowers, which are up to 12cm (5in) across, are green and white, and repay close inspection. The narrow side petals are sprinkled with tiny protuberances and are delicately haired, while the dorsal sepal is boldly striped with green and white. The pouches are glossy green with pronounced veining. Maudiae has attractive, mottled leaves - inherited from P. callosum - so needs warmer temperatures than some other paphiopedilums. Its mixed parentage means that flowers can appear in spring or summer.

QUICK REFERENCE

PLANT SIZE
Up to 30cm (12in) when in flower.

NUMBER OF FLOWERS
1 per stem.

FLOWERING PERIOD
Spring and summer.

REGULARITY OF FLOWERING
An established plant will flower regularly every year.

HABIT OF GROWTH
Evergreen sympodial orchid that does not have pseudobulbs.

BEST WAY TO GROW
Grow in a pot that restricts the roots and which contains terrestrial orchid compost with added bark chips.

GENERAL CARE
Intermediate growing (min 14-19ºC/57-66ºF; max 30-33ºC/86-91ºF). Shade from hot sun in summer; full light in winter. Water freely when in active growth, more sparingly in winter. Do not mist. Feed every 3 to 4 weeks when growing strongly from spring to summer.

PROPAGATION
Generally not suitable for division, although large plants can be divided with care when repotting.

EASE OF CULTIVATION
This plant needs some care to ensure even flower production.

Phragmipedium Magdalene Rose

Crossing Eric Young 'Rocket Fire' and Beauport 'Rose Flare' resulted in this hybrid, which was registered in 2001 by the Ackers Orchid Culture Garden Center of Wisconsin, USA. The red in the flower was inherited from Phragmipedium besseae, a stunning species found in Ecuador and Peru as recently as the early 1980s.

The flowers, approximately 7cm (2¾in) across, are a rich rose pink – a colour influenced by P. besseae, which can produce flowers in shades of red, orange, salmon, peach and yellow. The lips are stained yellow with reddish spotting within. The flowers are carried on tall stems that rise above a basal cluster of glossy, arching leaves. It is important that you use a moisture-retentive growing medium, so the roots never dry out.

QUICK REFERENCE

PLANT SIZE
Up to 45cm (18in).

NUMBER OF FLOWERS
Flowers are carried singly on tall stems or in short racemes of 2 or more.

FLOWERING PERIOD
Each flower spike can bloom over an 18-24-month period.

REGULARITY OF FLOWERING
A mature plant can be more or less permanently in bloom.

HABIT OF GROWTH
Evergreen sympodial orchid that does not have pseudobulbs.

BEST WAY TO GROW
Grow in a pot that restricts the roots and is filled with terrestrial orchid compost, preferably with added rockwool to help keep the roots moist.

GENERAL CARE
Intermediate growing (min 14-19ºC/57-66ºF; max 30-33ºC/ 86-91ºF). Shade from hot sun in summer; full light in winter. Water freely when in full growth and mist daily. Water more sparingly in winter, but the compost should not dry out. Feed every 3 to 4 weeks when the plant is in full growth.

PROPAGATION
Divide with care in late winter to early spring, before growth begins.

EASE OF CULTIVATION
Some experience required.

Phragmipedium Ralph Goldner

This orchid is a hybrid of Phragmipedium Memoria Dick Clements and P. Saint Ouen and was registered as recently as 2002. It was bred at the American nursery Woodstream Orchids, which specialises in slipper orchids.

The flowers, which are up to 7cm (2¾in) across, are a clear delicate pink. The fine markings are most clearly seen when they are backlit. This plant makes a fine contrast to some of the more richly coloured phragmipediums and rightly excites both breeders and growers. Using a fine-grade compost or rockwool makes sure the roots stay relatively wet – this is important for phragmipediums.

QUICK REFERENCE

PLANT SIZE
Up to 45cm (18in) when in flower.

NUMBER OF FLOWERS
2 or 3 per stem, though flowers can also be produced singly.

FLOWERING PERIOD
Flowers are produced in sequence, each flower spike blooming over a period of 18-24 months.

REGULARITY OF FLOWERING
A mature plant can be more or less permanently in flower.

HABIT OF GROWTH
Robust, fibrous-rooted evergreen sympodial orchid without pseudobulbs.

BEST WAY TO GROW
Grow in a pot that restricts the roots and contains terrestrial or fine-grade epiphytic orchid compost, preferably with added rockwool to help keep the roots moist.

GENERAL CARE
Intermediate growing (min 14-19°C/57-66°F; max 30-33°C/86-91°F). Shade from hot sun in summer; full light in winter. Water freely when in full growth and mist daily; water more sparingly in winter. Feed every 3 to 4 weeks when in active growth.

PROPAGATION
Divide with care in late winter to early spring, before growth begins.

EASE OF CULTIVATION
Some experience required.

phalaenopsis

In the wild, Phalaenopsis - the moth orchid - ranges throughout tropical southeast Asia. These plants have always been popular, but extensive breeding with the related Doritis over the last 20 years has taken them to a new level. No other group produces flowers so reliably over such a long period, and the colour range is phenomenal. They are also more tolerant of dry atmospheres than other orchids and as such are virtually indestructible. While they can be in flower virtually all year round, a short winter rest - kept cool with minimal water - will do them good. If a plant stops flowering, give it a rest for a few weeks in cool conditions to restore its vigour. The one possible drawback for amateurs is the difficulty of propagation.

Phalaenopsis Anthura Boston

Anthura BV is a large commercial nursery in the Netherlands that specialises in anthuriums, bromeliads and phalaenopsis - all intended to be grown as houseplants. As such, they do not appear in the International Orchid Register. The Anthura hybrids are often seen for sale in garden centres, DIY stores and other outlets that do not specialise in orchids.

Boston is one of a series of hybrids that are named in honour of various major cities around the world. Its warm lilac pink flowers, which are 8-10cm (3-4in) across, are delicately pencilled darker and have cherry pink lips. They are carried on arching stems well above the leaves, which are broad and of substantial texture. Stake the flower stems to just beneath the flower truss. Cutting back the flowers to a node immediately after they have faded but before the stem shows any sign of dieback should result in further flower production.

QUICK REFERENCE

PLANT SIZE
Up to 60cm (24in) when in flower.

NUMBER OF FLOWERS
Up to 10 or more per flower stem.

FLOWERING PERIOD
More or less continuous throughout the year.

REGULARITY OF FLOWERING
New flowering stems are produced every 6-8 weeks (slowing down in winter).

HABIT OF GROWTH
Evergreen monopodial orchid that does not have pseudobulbs.

BEST WAY TO GROW
Grow in a pot or slatted basket containing epiphytic orchid compost.

GENERAL CARE
Warm growing (min 20-24°C/68-75°F; max 30-33°C/ 86-91°F). Keep in a well-lit site all year, but screen from direct sun. Water throughout the year (less in winter, but keep the compost evenly moist). Mist the leaves daily in summer. Feed weekly year round, unless inducing dormancy.

PROPAGATION
Division is not usually possible. Keikis are occasionally produced.

EASE OF CULTIVATION
An easy orchid to grow as a houseplant.

Phalaenopsis Anthura Madrid

While the parentage of the Anthura hybrids is not publicly recorded, Madrid clearly shows the influence of Phalaenopsis amabilis, a beautiful epiphytic species found in a range from the Philippines and Indonesia through to Australia.

Like its ancestor, this plant has sparkling blush white flowers – in this case most delicately veined with pink and with orange-marked lips. Fully open, at about 9-11cm (31/2-41/2in) across, they are among the largest of any of the phalaenopsis. As a result, expect fewer per stem. For the most elegant effect, stake the flower stems to just beneath the flower truss, which should then arch outwards. Cut back flowered stems just above a node, not to the base, immediately after flowering but before the stem has started to die back. This will encourage the stem to branch and produce more flowers.

QUICK REFERENCE

PLANT SIZE
Up to 60cm (24in) when in flower.

NUMBER OF FLOWERS
Up to 10 or more per flower stem.

FLOWERING PERIOD
More or less continuous throughout the year.

REGULARITY OF FLOWERING
New flowering stems are produced every 6-8 weeks (slowing down in winter).

HABIT OF GROWTH
Evergreen monopodial orchid that does not have pseudobulbs.

BEST WAY TO GROW
Grow in a pot or slatted basket containing epiphytic orchid compost.

GENERAL CARE
Warm growing (min 20-24ºC/68-75ºF; max 30-33ºC/ 86-91ºF). Keep in a well-lit site all year, but screen from direct sun. Water throughout the year (less in winter, but keep the compost evenly moist). Mist the leaves daily in summer. Feed weekly year round, unless inducing dormancy.

PROPAGATION
Division is not usually possible. Keikis are occasionally produced.

EASE OF CULTIVATION
An easy orchid to grow as a houseplant.

Phalaenopsis Brother Pico Chip

A vast number of phalaenopsis hybrids have 'Brother' in the name, bred at the Brother Orchid Nursery in Taichung, Taiwan. This one was registered in 1998. Its parents are Phalaenopsis Petite Pink and the species P. stuartiana, an epiphyte found in the Philippines.

Genes inherited from the species have reduced the size of the flowers, which, at 7cm (2¾in) across, are somewhat smaller than many other phalaenopsis hybrids. The colour comes via the hybrid line, petals and sepals being a warm translucent pink, the lips somewhat darker and spotted with deep cerise pink. Stake the flower stems to just beneath the flower truss for the best effect. To maintain flower production cut back the flowered stems to a node before the stems start to die back.

QUICK REFERENCE

PLANT SIZE
Up to 45cm (18in) when in flower.

NUMBER OF FLOWERS
Up to 10 or more per flower stem.

FLOWERING PERIOD
More or less continuous throughout the year.

REGULARITY OF FLOWERING
New flowering stems are produced every 6-8 weeks (slowing down in winter).

HABIT OF GROWTH
Evergreen monopodial orchid that does not have pseudobulbs.

BEST WAY TO GROW
Grow in a a pot or slatted basket containing epiphytic orchid compost.

GENERAL CARE
Warm growing (min 20-24°C/68-75°F; max 30-33°C/ 86-91°F). Keep in a well-lit site all year, but screen from direct sun. Water throughout the year (less in winter, but keep the compost evenly moist). Mist the leaves daily in summer. Feed weekly year round, unless inducing dormancy.

PROPAGATION
Division is not usually possible. Keikis are occasionally produced.

EASE OF CULTIVATION
An easy orchid to grow as a houseplant.

Phalaenopsis Brother Pico Circle

Another hybrid from the Brother stable, Brother Pico Circle was registered in 1998. Its parents are Phalaenopsis Brother Delight and P. Baby Angel.

The flamboyant style of the flowers, which are carried rather densely on the stems, represents a significant trend in phalaenopsis breeding. Large and rounded, up to 8cm (3in) across or more and ranked close on the stems, they are a warm pink, freely spotted with darker pink. The lips are a warm cherry red. Stake the flower stems to keep them upright. To keep up flower production, cut back trusses to a node lower down on the stems once the flowers have faded but before the stems have started to die back.

QUICK REFERENCE

PLANT SIZE
Up to 60cm (24in) when in flower.

NUMBER OF FLOWERS
Up to 10 or more per flower stem.

FLOWERING PERIOD
More or less continuous throughout the year.

REGULARITY OF FLOWERING
New flowering stems are produced every 6-8 weeks (slowing down in winter).

HABIT OF GROWTH
Evergreen monopodial orchid that does not have pseudobulbs.

BEST WAY TO GROW
Grow in a pot or slatted basket containing epiphytic orchid compost.

GENERAL CARE
Warm growing (min 20-24°C/68-75°F; max 30-33°C/ 86-91°F). Keep in a well-lit site all year, but screen from direct sun. Water throughout the year (less in winter, but keep the compost evenly moist). Mist the leaves daily in summer. Feed weekly year round, unless inducing dormancy.

PROPAGATION
Division is not usually possible. Keikis are occasionally produced.

EASE OF CULTIVATION
An easy orchid to grow as a houseplant.

Phalaenopsis Dragon's Charm

Dragon's Charm was registered in 1989, and is a cross between Phalaenopsis Taipei Gold and P. Barbara Moler. The petals and sepals are rather narrower and more pointed than some other phalaenopsis hybrids – that and the rather unusual old gold colouring give this orchid a certain distinction.

The flowers, which are about 7cm (2¾in) across, are lightly barred and spotted with red towards the base. The lips are marked with orange-red. Stake the flower stems to just beneath the flower truss for the best effect.

Cut back the flower trusses once the flowers have faded but before the stems have started to die back. This will encourage further flower stems to be produced.

QUICK REFERENCE

PLANT SIZE
Up to 60cm (24in) when in flower.

NUMBER OF FLOWERS
Up to 10 or more per flower stem.

FLOWERING PERIOD
More or less continuous throughout the year.

REGULARITY OF FLOWERING
New flowering stems are produced every 6-8 weeks (slowing down in winter).

HABIT OF GROWTH
Evergreen monopodial orchid that does not have pseudobulbs.

BEST WAY TO GROW
Grow in a pot or slatted basket containing epiphytic orchid compost.

GENERAL CARE
Warm growing (min 20-24ºC/68-75ºF; max 30-33ºC/ 86-91ºF). Keep in a well-lit site all year, but screen from direct sun. Water throughout the year (less in winter, but keep the compost evenly moist). Mist the leaves daily in summer. Feed weekly year round, unless inducing dormancy.

PROPAGATION
Division is not usually possible. Keikis are occasionally produced.

EASE OF CULTIVATION
An easy orchid to grow as a houseplant.

Phalaenopsis Dutch Starlight

This hybrid was registered in 1994 as a cross between Doritaenopsis Connie Bowers and Phalaenopsis stuartiana, an epiphytic species from the Philippines. Doritaenopsis is a bigeneric hybrid of Doritis, an Indo-Malayan genus comprising a mere two species, and Phalaenopsis.

Dutch Starlight has flowers of a clear, sparkling white, up to 8cm (3in) across with broad, almost rounded petals. The lips are marked with yellow and spotted with red. Overall, the plant is more compact than many other modern phalaenopsis hybrids, making it an ideal choice if space is limited. Stake stems up to just below the flower truss. To ensure even flowering, cut back stems just above a node once the flowers have faded, but before the stems have started to die back.

QUICK REFERENCE

PLANT SIZE

Up to 30cm (12in) when in flower.

NUMBER OF FLOWERS

Up to 10 or more per flower stem.

FLOWERING PERIOD

More or less continuous throughout the year.

REGULARITY OF FLOWERING

New flowering stems are produced every 6-8 weeks (slowing down in winter).

HABIT OF GROWTH

Evergreen monopodial orchid that does not have pseudobulbs.

BEST WAY TO GROW

Grow in a pot or slatted basket containing epiphytic orchid compost.

GENERAL CARE

Warm growing (min 20-24ºC/68-75ºF; max 30-33ºC/ 86-91ºF). Keep in a well-lit site all year, but screen from direct sun. Water throughout the year (less in winter, but keep the compost evenly moist). Mist the leaves daily in summer. Feed weekly year round, unless inducing dormancy.

PROPAGATION

Division is not usually possible. Keikis are occasionally produced.

EASE OF CULTIVATION

An easy orchid to grow as a houseplant.

Phalaenopsis Ever-spring Light

This hybrid's curious name reflects its breeder, Ever Spring Orchids, which is based in Winnipeg, Canada. The nursery specialises in phalaenopsis. The plant was registered in 1992, as a cross between Phalaenopsis Ever-spring Star and P. Golden Peoker.

The flowers are much smaller than those of many other phalaenopsis, and overall the plant has a dainty appearance. Up to 5cm (2in) across, the flowers are white, irregularly blotched with a glowing clear red. Stake stems to keep them upright. Cut back flowered stems just above a node, not to the base. This will encourage the stem to branch and produce more flowers.

QUICK REFERENCE

PLANT SIZE
Up to 60cm (24in) when in flower.

NUMBER OF FLOWERS
Up to 10 or more per flower stem.

FLOWERING PERIOD
More or less continuous throughout the year.

REGULARITY OF FLOWERING
New flowering stems are produced every 6-8 weeks (slowing down in winter).

HABIT OF GROWTH
Evergreen monopodial orchid that does not have pseudobulbs.

BEST WAY TO GROW
Grow in a pot or slatted basket containing epiphytic orchid compost.

GENERAL CARE
Warm growing (min 20-24ºC/68-75ºF; max 30-33ºC/ 86-91ºF). Keep in a well-lit site all year, but screen from direct sun. Water throughout the year (less in winter, but keep the compost evenly moist). Mist the leaves daily in summer. Feed weekly year round, unless inducing dormancy.

PROPAGATION
Division is not usually possible. Keikis are occasionally produced.

EASE OF CULTIVATION
An easy orchid to grow as a houseplant.

Phalaenopsis Lava Flow

Lava Flow was registered in 1993 by Orchid Zone/Hager, its parents being Phalaenopsis Red Knight and P. Golden Buddha. The name Lava Flow has - quite legitimately - been given to some other orchid hybrids, so make sure when ordering this plant that it is a phalaenopsis you will be getting.

Golden Buddha has been much used in phalaenopsis breeding, but the flowers of Lava Flow, which are up to 8cm (3in) across, owe more to its other parent, as they are a uniform glowing cerise pink. Stake stems to keep them upright. To maintain flower production, cut back flowered stems just above a node but before the stems have started to die back.

QUICK REFERENCE

PLANT SIZE
Up to 60cm (24in) when in flower.

NUMBER OF FLOWERS
Up to 10 or more per flower stem.

FLOWERING PERIOD
More or less continuous throughout the year.

REGULARITY OF FLOWERING
New flowering stems are produced every 6-8 weeks (slowing down in winter).

HABIT OF GROWTH
Evergreen monopodial orchid that does not have pseudobulbs.

BEST WAY TO GROW
Grow in a pot or slatted basket containing epiphytic orchid compost.

GENERAL CARE
Warm growing (min 20-24°C/68-75°F; max 30-33°C/ 86-91°F). Keep in a well-lit site all year, but screen from direct sun. Water throughout the year (less in winter, but keep the compost evenly moist). Mist the leaves daily in summer. Feed weekly year round, unless inducing dormancy.

PROPAGATION
Division is not usually possible. Keikis are occasionally produced.

EASE OF CULTIVATION
An easy orchid to grow as a houseplant.

Phalaenopsis Lippeflair

Lippeflair is a hybrid of German origin, bred by Hark Orchideen of Lippstadt – Lipperose, Lippewunder and Lippegruss being among its stablemates. This nursery specialises in phalaenopsis. The pink flowers produced by the breeder were regarded as something of a breakthrough when they first appeared.

The flowers open to 8cm (3in) across, petals and sepals showing an even, warm lilac pink coloration. The lips are generously spotted with maroon, with yellow towards the base. Stake stems up to just below the flower truss. Cut back flowered stems just above a node, not to the base. This will encourage the stems to branch and produce more flowers.

QUICK REFERENCE

PLANT SIZE
Up to 45cm (18in) when in flower.

NUMBER OF FLOWERS
Up to 10 or more per flower stem.

FLOWERING PERIOD
More or less continuous throughout the year.

REGULARITY OF FLOWERING
New flowering stems are produced every 6-8 weeks (slowing down in winter).

HABIT OF GROWTH
Evergreen monopodial orchid that does not have pseudobulbs.

BEST WAY TO GROW
Grow in a pot or slatted basket containing epiphytic orchid compost.

GENERAL CARE
Warm growing (min 20-24°C/68-75°F; max 30-33°C/ 86-91°F). Keep in a well-lit site all year, but screen from direct sun. Water throughout the year (less in winter, but keep the compost evenly moist). Mist the leaves daily in summer. Feed weekly year round, unless inducing dormancy.

PROPAGATION
Division is not usually possible. Keikis are occasionally produced.

EASE OF CULTIVATION
An easy orchid to grow as a houseplant.

Phalaenopsis Malibu Bistro

The grex Malibu Bistro was registered in 1998, having been bred from Phalaenopsis Prince Puck and P. Kathleen Ai at the Zuma Canyon Nursery in America – which specialises in phalaenopsis breeding.

The flowers are typical of modern moth orchids, with broad, rounded petals and somewhat narrower sepals. In coloration they are similar, being a soft rose pink with very clear pencilling in warm lilac purple. The pencilling is thicker on the lips, and there are the expected yellow markings towards the centre. The flowers are large too, up to 9cm (31/2in) wide when fully open, appearing crowded on the stems. Stake stems up to just below the flower truss. Cut back flowered stems to a node lower down to encourage further flowering.

QUICK REFERENCE

PLANT SIZE
Up to 60cm (24in) when in flower.

NUMBER OF FLOWERS
Up to 10 or more per flower stem.

FLOWERING PERIOD
More or less continuous throughout the year.

REGULARITY OF FLOWERING
New flowering stems are produced every 6-8 weeks (slowing down in winter).

HABIT OF GROWTH
Evergreen monopodial orchid that does not have pseudobulbs.

BEST WAY TO GROW
Grow in a pot or slatted basket containing epiphytic orchid compost.

GENERAL CARE
Warm growing (min 20-24ºC/68-75ºF; max 30-33ºC/ 86-91ºF). Keep in a well-lit site all year, but screen from direct sun. Water throughout the year (less in winter, but keep the compost evenly moist). Mist the leaves daily in summer. Feed weekly year round, unless inducing dormancy.

PROPAGATION
Division is not usually possible. Keikis are occasionally produced.

EASE OF CULTIVATION
An easy orchid to grow as a houseplant.

other species and hybrids

This chapter comprises a range of interesting orchid species and hybrids that do not fit into any of the other larger groups. Two important genera appear here - the pleiones, from the Far East, which are virtually hardy enough to be grown as garden plants in some areas, and the South American miltoniopsis an attractive group referred to as 'pansy' orchids. Miltoniopsis and the related Miltonia will breed with odontoglossums but are distinct, and most modern breeding programmes have focused on developing a relatively pure line of plants with delightfully coloured flowers.

While some of the following are connoisseur's plants, others are suitable for more general collectors.

Brassia Arania Verde

This striking hybrid was registered in 1990 by the breeder Pendleton. It was the progeny of a cross between Brassia Rex, an orchid that has been widely used in breeding programmes, and B. gireoudiana, a species from Costa Rica and Panama.

Brassias are often referred to as spider orchids, because of the shape of the flowers. Carried in arching sprays, with narrow, ribbon-like petals and sepals of a greenish cream strongly barred with brownish maroon, they do indeed resemble spiders, stretching to 10cm (4in) across and airily suspended above the leaves. The prominent lips are cream with maroon blotches. Like all the brassias, Arania Verde is a striking plant that is sure to become a talking point.

QUICK REFERENCE

PLANT SIZE
Up to 50cm (20in) when in flower.

NUMBER OF FLOWERS
10-12 per stem.

FLOWERING PERIOD
Spring.

REGULARITY OF FLOWERING
Annually.

HABIT OF GROWTH
Evergreen sympodial orchid with plum-shaped pseudobulbs.

BEST WAY TO GROW
Grow in a pot or basket filled with epiphytic orchid compost. Alternatively, tie to a piece of bark.

GENERAL CARE
Intermediate growing (min 14-19°C/57-66°F; max 30-33°C/86-91°F). Shade from direct light in summer; full light in winter. Water freely when in active growth in spring and summer and mist daily. Water sparingly in winter. Feed every 3 to 4 weeks when in active growth.

PROPAGATION
Divide after flowering, potting up backbulbs separately.

EASE OF CULTIVATION
A fairly easy hybrid for amateurs.

Bulbophyllum careyanum

Bulbophyllums – a genus of possibly as many as 1,200 species – are found in a variety of habitats in tropical and subtropical regions. They occur mainly in Asia, with some in Africa and Australia. B. careyanum itself occurs in the eastern Himalaya, Burma and Thailand, where it grows epiphytically.

Each pseudobulb of this plant produces a solitary leaf. The flowers, which are only 0.2cm (1/12in) across, appear in summer in arching racemes. They are orange-yellow or greenish, tinged with reddish green or purple, and the lips are violet purple. The flowers of this species are sweetly scented – those of some other bulbophyllums can have a decidedly unpleasant scent. The plant needs a complete rest over winter, though it may be necessary to mist the pseudobulbs from time to time if they appear to be shrivelling – to ensure they remain plump and able to produce fresh growth in spring.

QUICK REFERENCE

PLANT SIZE
Up to 25cm (10in).

NUMBER OF FLOWERS
Up to 100 or more per stem.

FLOWERING PERIOD
Usually summer, though it can also produce flowers at other times.

REGULARITY OF FLOWERING
Annually.

HABIT OF GROWTH
Evergreen sympodial orchid with spherical to egg-shaped pseudobulbs.

BEST WAY TO GROW
Grow in a shallow pot or basket filled with epiphytic orchid compost; alternatively, mount on bark.

GENERAL CARE
Cool growing (min 10-13ºC/50-55ºF; max 21-24ºC/ 70-75ºF). Grow in partial shade in summer; full light in winter. Water freely in spring/summer and mist daily. Keep dry in winter. Feed every 3 to 4 weeks when in active growth.

PROPAGATION
Divide a congested plant in spring or immediately after flowering.

EASE OF CULTIVATION
Some care needed for success.

Cirrhopetalum picturatum

This tropical Indian species is sometimes listed under Bulbophyllum. The genus occurs in tropical and subtropical regions, mainly in Asia, C. picturatum being found in India.

Each pseudobulb generally produces only a single leaf. The erect flowering stems are speckled with purple. The fragrant flowers, carried in umbrella-like clusters on stems that arise from the base of the plant, can appear at any time of year and are up to 4cm (11/2in) long. The dorsal sepal, dull green and spotted with crimson, has soft, pimple-like protuberances. Lateral sepals are long, narrow, pale green and hang down. The petals show a similar colour but are broader. The fleshy lips are crimson. This species is relatively rare in collections.

QUICK REFERENCE

PLANT SIZE
About 25cm (10in) tall when in flower.

NUMBER OF FLOWERS
Flowers are produced in clusters of 7 or more.

FLOWERING PERIOD
Various times of year.

REGULARITY OF FLOWERING
At least twice a year.

HABIT OF GROWTH
Evergreen sympodial orchid with creeping rhizomes, on which the rounded pseudobulbs are widely spaced.

BEST WAY TO GROW
Grow in a shallow pot or basket filled with epiphytic orchid compost. Alternatively, attach to a piece of bark.

GENERAL CARE
Intermediate growing (min 14-19ºC/57-66ºF; max 30-33ºC/86-91ºF). Grow in partial shade in summer; full light in winter. Water freely in spring/summer and mist daily. Keep dry in winter. Feed every 3 to 4 weeks when in active growth.

PROPAGATION
Divide a congested plant in spring or immediately after flowering.

EASE OF CULTIVATION
Suitable for experienced growers only.

Dendrochilum glumaceum

Dendrochilum – a genus of epiphytic evergreens that has the delightful common name of golden chain orchid – is found at high altitudes in southeast Asia and New Guinea. In the wild the species grows on rocks as well as on trees, always near rivers. D. glumaceum is from the Philippines.

At 2cm (3/4in) across the star-like, white to ivory flowers are not large, but are produced in great quantity – densely crowded in two rows on arching stems that emerge from the centre of the new growth. They do not open wide but nevertheless give off a sweet fragrance, the whole effect being of a chain of flowers. The lips are pale green. This is one of the most popular members of the genus – and deservedly so.

QUICK REFERENCE

PLANT SIZE
Up to 50cm (20in).

NUMBER OF FLOWERS
Up to 100 or more per stem.

FLOWERING PERIOD
Usually early summer, though flowers can also be produced at other times of the year.

REGULARITY OF FLOWERING
An established plant will flower every year.

HABIT OF GROWTH
Evergreen sympodial orchid that has ovoid to cylindrical pseudobulbs.

BEST WAY TO GROW
Grow in a container filled with epiphytic orchid compost.

GENERAL CARE
Cool growing (min 10-13ºC/50-55ºF; max 21-24ºC/ 70-75ºF). Shade from direct sun in summer; full light in winter. Water freely and mist daily when in active growth; water very sparingly in winter. Feed every 3 to 4 weeks when in active growth.

PROPAGATION
Divide when the plant fills the pot; dormant backbulbs can be potted up separately.

EASE OF CULTIVATION
Some experience required.

Doritaenopsis Aposya

Doritis is a small genus of possibly no more than two species, native to Indo-Malaya. The plants show some affinity with Phalaenopsis, and have been hybridised with them to produce Doritaenopsis.

Though it looks like a phalaenopsis at first glance, Aposya is a much daintier plant with elegant flowers that are well spaced and held on tall, straight stems. At 4cm (11/2in) across, they are a bright fuchsia pink with prominent, spear-shaped red lips that point forward – a feature that betrays the plant's Doritis parentage.

QUICK REFERENCE

PLANT SIZE
Up to 45cm (18in) when in flower.

NUMBER OF FLOWERS
12 or more per stem.

FLOWERING PERIOD
Can flower intermittently throughout the year, but is usually most prolific in summer.

REGULARITY OF FLOWERING
The plant is seldom without flowers.

HABIT OF GROWTH
Evergreen monopodial orchid that does not have pseudobulbs.

BEST WAY TO GROW
Grow in a container of epiphytic compost or attached to a piece of bark.

GENERAL CARE
Warm growing (min 20-24°C/68-75°F; max 30-33°C/ 86-91°F). Grow in bright filtered light throughout the year. Water frequently when in strong growth and mist daily. Reduce watering in winter but do not allow to dry out completely. Feed every 3 to 4 weeks when in strong growth from spring to summer.

PROPAGATION
Division is not normally possible, though the plant may occasionally produce keikis.

EASE OF CULTIVATION
This plant is worth trying if you can grow phalaenopsis successfully.

Dryadella zebrina

Dryadellas are dwarf orchids found in Central and South America. D. zebrina is a rare species from Brazil, showing some affinity with Masdevallia. Some of the species grow lithophytically – in other words, on or among rocks. D. zebrina is of diminutive size and is likely to appeal to dedicated collectors only.

The flower stems are short, while the leaves are erect or slightly spreading. The flowers, which are approximately 2cm (3⁄4in) across, are carried individually. The cupped sepals are cream and densely spotted with purplish black or grey. The petals can be cream or maroon, while the lips are greyish white. A distinguishing feature of the sepals is their long tail-like extensions, which can also be observed in some of the masdevallias. The linear leaves are tufted and of a dark green colour.

QUICK REFERENCE

PLANT SIZE
Up to 8cm (3in).

NUMBER OF FLOWERS
Usually 1 per stem.

FLOWERING PERIOD
Usually late winter to early spring.

REGULARITY OF FLOWERING
An established plant will flower every year.

HABIT OF GROWTH
Evergreen sympodial epiphytic orchid without pseudobulbs.

BEST WAY TO GROW
Grow in a small pot of fine-grade epiphytic orchid compost.

GENERAL CARE
Cool growing (min 10-13ºC/50-55ºF; max 21-24ºC/ 70-75ºF). Shade from direct sun in summer; full light in winter. Water freely when in growth and mist daily. Reduce watering in winter but do not allow to dry out completely. Feed every 3 to 4 weeks from spring to summer.

PROPAGATION
Generally unsuitable for division, though cuttings may sometimes be successful.

EASE OF CULTIVATION
Some experience required for success.

Lepanthopsis astrophora 'Stalky'

Lepanthopsis astrophora is an exquisite, but variable, miniature species from tropical areas of Central and South America. It is widely distributed in Venezuela, at altitudes of 700–1,635m (2,300–5,360ft). The specific epithet means 'star-bearing', referring to the appearance of the inflorescence. The genus shows some affinity with Lepanthes and the somewhat more familiar Pleurothallis. It is rare in cultivation. 'Stalky' is a selected form.

The leaves are leathery but smooth in texture. The star-like, bright rose-purple flowers, which are about 1cm (1/2in) across and lightly studded with pimple-like protuberances, are carried on racemes that can extend to 12cm (5in). This is a jewel-like plant, but perhaps for dedicated growers only. For the best results, repot annually in the autumn or spring.

QUICK REFERENCE

PLANT SIZE
Up to 12cm (5in) tall when in flower.

NUMBER OF FLOWERS
Up to 10 flowers or more per raceme.

FLOWERING PERIOD
Usually late winter to early spring, though the plant can also flower at other times.

REGULARITY OF FLOWERING
An established plant can flower several times per year.

HABIT OF GROWTH
Creeping, evergreen sympodial orchid with tiny rhizomes.

BEST WAY TO GROW
Grow in a small pot filled with fine-grade epiphytic orchid compost.

GENERAL CARE
Cool growing (min 10–13ºC/50–55ºF; max 21–24ºC/ 70–75ºF) to intermediate growing (min 14–19ºC/ 57–66ºF; max 30–33ºC/ 86–91ºF). Shade from direct sun in summer; full light in winter. Water freely when in active growth and mist daily. Water more sparingly at other times. Feed every 3 to 4 weeks when in strong growth.

PROPAGATION
Divide the rhizomes with care, immediately after flowering.

EASE OF CULTIVATION
Suitable for experienced growers only.

Ludisia discolor

This plant is a real curiosity. Ludisia herself remains a woman of some mystery – she is apparently the subject of an ancient Greek eulogy penned by her widower. The orchid named in her honour is found in China and southeast Asia, growing on the mossy banks of rivers and sometimes among rocks. It is one of a number of species referred to as 'jewel' orchids, on account of the leaf coloration.

Almost uniquely, this plant is grown for its foliage rather than its flowers. The leaves, which can be up to 12cm (5in) long, are a rich, dark, velvety green – some can appear chocolate brown, bronze or even black. They are eye-catchingly veined with shimmering golden yellow to copper red. The intricate white and yellow flowers, only 1cm (1⁄2in) across and with distinctive twisted lips, hover above the plant on tall stems in quantity, like small insects. This is certainly a beautiful plant. A low light level is critical – too much light and the leaves turn a pinkish brown.

QUICK REFERENCE

PLANT SIZE
Up to 10cm (4in), more when in flower.

NUMBER OF FLOWERS
Each stem produces 10 or more flowers.

FLOWERING PERIOD
Flowers can be produced at various times during the year.

REGULARITY OF FLOWERING
The plant should flower regularly if it is divided after flowering.

HABIT OF GROWTH
Evergreen terrestrial orchid with creeping, fleshy rhizomes.

BEST WAY TO GROW
Grow in a container filled with terrestrial orchid compost or a mix of leafmould, coir, bark and charcoal.

GENERAL CARE
Intermediate growing (min 14-19ºC/57-66ºF; max 30-33ºC/ 86-91ºF). Shade from direct light at all times. Water freely throughout the year and mist daily during warm weather. Feed every 3 to 4 weeks when in active growth.

PROPAGATION
Divide after flowering, making sure each new division shows signs of fresh growth.

EASE OF CULTIVATION
Some experience required.

Maxillaria arachnites

This species, a member of the lepidota alliance, hails from Venezuela, Colombia and Ecuador. Arachnites pertains to arachnids - and the flowers do perch among the leaves like spiders.

The flowers are intriguing rather than beautiful. Up to 9cm (31/2in) across, they have narrow, yellow-green sepals and white petals, the whole structure being flushed with maroon. The golden-yellow lips are finely toothed at the edges. It is the delicious scent that makes the plant so worthwhile. The substantial, grassy leaves are up to 25cm (10in) in length. This species is unusual in collections, but it is worth seeking out if you like fragrant orchids.

QUICK REFERENCE

PLANT SIZE
Around 20cm (8in) when in flower.

NUMBER OF FLOWERS
1 per stem.

FLOWERING PERIOD
Mainly during the summer, though flowers can also be produced at other times.

REGULARITY OF FLOWERING
Intermittent.

HABIT OF GROWTH
Evergreen sympodial orchid with small pseudobulbs (some maxiallarias do not have pseudobulbs).

BEST WAY TO GROW
Grow in a pot or, probably better, hanging basket filled with epiphytic compost.

GENERAL CARE
Cool growing (min 10-13ºC/50-55ºF; max 21-24ºC/ 70-75ºF) to intermediate growing (min 14-19ºC/ 57-66ºF; max 30-33ºC/ 86-91ºF). Shade from direct light in summer; full light in winter. Water throughout the year and mist daily in spring and summer. Feed every 3 to 4 weeks when in active growth.

PROPAGATION
Divide when the roots emerge around the top of the container.

EASE OF CULTIVATION
Some experience required.

Maxillaria lexarzana

One of those orchids that exercises the minds of botanists and taxonomists, Maxillaria lexarzana is part of the cucullata alliance – members of which are often misidentified. M. cucullata itself is a highly variable epiphytic species in the wild, which leads to much dispute. You may sometimes come across this orchid – or similar ones – sold under the name M. cucullata.

This plant tolerates a wider temperature range than some other orchid species. The flowers are up to 2.5cm (1in) across and intriguing rather than beautiful – but repay close inspection. Petals and sepals are a dingy brownish red, while the lips are dark purplish red – though colours can vary, and plants with yellow or pink flowers are not unknown. This is definitely an orchid for the dedicated grower, perhaps as part of a collection of cucullata types.

QUICK REFERENCE

PLANT SIZE

Up to 15cm (6in).

NUMBER OF FLOWERS

Flowers are produced singly on stems or occasionally in small clusters.

FLOWERING PERIOD

Usually summer to autumn, but plants in cultivation can also flower at other times.

REGULARITY OF FLOWERING

Flowers appear intermittently over a long period.

HABIT OF GROWTH

Evergreen sympodial orchid with small, oval pseudobulbs (some maxillarias do not have pseudobulbs).

BEST WAY TO GROW

Grow in a pot or hanging basket filled with epiphytic compost. Also suitable for tying to a piece of bark.

GENERAL CARE

Cool growing (min 10-13ºC/50-55ºF; max 21-24ºC/ 70-75ºF) to intermediate growing (min 14-19ºC/ 57-66ºF; max 30-33ºC/ 86-91ºF). Shade from direct light in summer, place in full light in winter. Water throughout the year and mist daily in spring and summer. Feed every 3 to 4 weeks when in active growth.

PROPAGATION

Divide when the roots emerge around the top of the container.

EASE OF CULTIVATION

A suitable species for a beginner.

Maxillaria picta

Maxillaria picta is a species from Brazil, where it is widely distributed on coastal mountains - generally above 700m (2,000ft). Though it is usually epiphytic it can also be found on rocks, often producing large clumps.

The flowers, which are up to 4cm (11/2in) across, are showier than those of many orchid species. They are also deliciously scented - in fact, this is one of the best of all orchid species in that respect, and a single flower can fill a room with fragrance. The waxy-textured sepals and slightly shorter petals are deep yellow inside, rather paler on the exterior and are gently curving towards their tips. They can be banded and/or flecked with purple, dark red or brown. The lips are yellowish white or cream and are spotted with red. This is a compact species, with two leaves on each pseudobulb.

QUICK REFERENCE

PLANT SIZE
Around 23cm (9in).

NUMBER OF FLOWERS
Flowers are carried singly on stems produced from the base.

FLOWERING PERIOD
Usually summer to autumn, but plants in cultivation can also flower at other times.

REGULARITY OF FLOWERING
Annually; once established, flowers will be produced in abundance.

HABIT OF GROWTH
Evergreen sympodial orchid with small, oval pseudobulbs (some maxiallarias do not have pseudobulbs).

BEST WAY TO GROW
Grow in a pot or hanging basket filled with epiphytic compost. Also suitable for tying to a piece of bark.

GENERAL CARE
Cool growing (min 10-13°C/50-55°F; max 21-24°C/ 70-75°F) to intermediate growing (min 14-19°C/ 57-66°F; max 30-33°C/ 86-91°F). Shade from direct light in summer, place in full light in winter. Water throughout the year and mist daily in spring and summer. Feed every 3 to 4 weeks when in active growth.

PROPAGATION
Divide when the roots emerge around the top of the container.

EASE OF CULTIVATION
This is one of the easiest species for beginners to grow.

Miltonia Enchra

Registered in 1970 this hybrid has been around for some time, but is found only rarely in collections. Its parents are Miltonia Pulchra and the species M. endresii (now Miltoniopsis warscewiczii), a winter-flowering species from Costa Rica that was introduced in 1830. The plant's rather strange name is a conflation of the two parents' names.

Opening flat to 8cm (3in) across, the flowers are a soft blush white, delightfully flared with a rich, deep pink. The lips have yellow centres.

Orchids of this type are now more generally classified as Miltoniopsis – the genus Miltonia has been greatly reduced in size.

QUICK REFERENCE

PLANT SIZE
Up to 30cm (12in).

NUMBER OF FLOWERS
Up to 5 or 6 per stem.

FLOWERING PERIOD
Flowers can be produced at various times of the year.

REGULARITY OF FLOWERING
Intermittent.

HABIT OF GROWTH
Evergreen sympodial orchid that has oval pseudobulbs.

BEST WAY TO GROW
Grow in a pot or hanging basket filled with epiphytic compost, or attached to a piece of bark.

GENERAL CARE
Cool growing (min 10-13ºC/50-55ºF; max 21-24ºC/ 70-75ºF). Grow in a shady position. Water year round, but avoid wetting the leaves. Do not mist. Feed every 3 to 4 weeks when the plant is in active growth.

PROPAGATION
Divide when the plant becomes congested.

EASE OF CULTIVATION
Some care needed for success.

Miltoniopsis Herralexandre

Miltoniopsis are the so-called pansy orchids, due to their appealing pansy-like 'faces'. They are closely related to, though distinct from, Miltonia. The parents of Herralexandre are Alexandre Dumas and Herrenhausen; it was registered in 1992 by the Beall Orchid Company of Washington State.

Miltoniopsis hybrids are more or less permanently in growth, the flower spikes appearing as the pseudobulbs mature. The flowers, which are up to 10cm (4in) across, are white with a rich purple and yellow 'mask' (actually, it is the broad, flaring lip that carries most of the contrasting colours). Sweetly fragrant, the flowers can last for five or six weeks on the plant – but are unsuitable for cutting and wilt rapidly in water. Though cool growing, miltoniopsis prefer being kept to the warmer end of the ranges.

QUICK REFERENCE

PLANT SIZE
Up to 30cm (12in).

NUMBER OF FLOWERS
Up to 6 per stem.

FLOWERING PERIOD
Usually spring to summer, with a second flowering in autumn.

REGULARITY OF FLOWERING
Can flower twice a year.

HABIT OF GROWTH
Evergreen, sympodial orchid with fleshy, ovoid pseudobulbs.

BEST WAY TO GROW
Grow in a small pot that restricts the roots and which contains epiphytic orchid compost.

GENERAL CARE
Cool growing (min 10-13°C/50-55°F; max 21-24°C/ 70-75°F). Grow in a shady position. Water year round, but avoid wetting the leaves. Do not mist. Feed every 3 to 4 weeks when the plant is in active growth.

PROPAGATION
Divide when the plant fills the container.

EASE OF CULTIVATION
Some care needed for success.

Pleione formosana

This beautiful orchid comes from wet wooded areas at high altitude in eastern China and Taiwan, where it is sometimes found growing lithophytically – among rocks. It is almost hardy. With luck, you could grow it in a sheltered, shady rockery outdoors – failing that, it's a good plant for an unheated alpine house.

The solitary flowers – which, at 8cm (3in) across, are large in size relative to the plant – are a warm pinkish-lilac. The lips, paler and trumpet-like, are fringed at the edges and marked inside with yellow and brown. This is a plant of quiet and refined beauty. Pleiones have not been extensively hybridised, though P. formosa has been crossed with P. humilis to produce the somewhat more flamboyant Eiger. This plant benefits from a winter rest. As the leaves start to die back in autumn, water only to keep the compost just moist. In winter, watering can cease altogether and the temperature can be allowed to drop to freezing point or just above.

QUICK REFERENCE

PLANT SIZE
Up to 15cm (6in).

NUMBER OF FLOWERS
Flowers are usually borne singly.

FLOWERING PERIOD
Spring.

REGULARITY OF FLOWERING
Annually.

HABIT OF GROWTH
Deciduous sympodial orchid that has rounded pseudobulbs.

BEST WAY TO GROW
Best in a shallow pan containing either epiphytic or terrestrial orchid compost.

GENERAL CARE
Half hardy (min 0ºC/32ºF), but probably able to withstand short periods below freezing point provided the roots are not wet. Shade from direct sun in summer; full light in winter. Water freely when in active growth and mist daily. Keep dry in winter. Feed every 3 to 4 weeks when in active growth.

PROPAGATION
Divide annually, in spring. Old pseudobulbs are best discarded.

EASE OF CULTIVATION
One of the easiest of the pleiones for a beginner to grow.

Pleione formosana var. alba

This is the naturally occurring white form of the preceding species (see page 183). It is something of a rarity in collections, and plants are thus highly prized. Each pseudobulb produces a single, folded leaf.

Pleiones were popular as subjects for corsages in the 1970s. Nowadays the phalaenopsis reign supreme, but this exquisite white form of pleione, with flowers up to 8cm (3in) across, could well form a subject for a discreet but stylish bridal bouquet, or maybe for a man's buttonhole. Petals and sepals flare backwards to showcase appealingly fringed trumpet-like lips that are boldly stained with yellow within. If you dare grow this outside, be sure to choose a sheltered spot and protect the flowers from mud splashes with a sheet of glass. Otherwise, it is probably best to grow pleiones in an alpine house. Most indoor rooms are too warm.

QUICK REFERENCE

PLANT SIZE
Up to 30cm (12in).

NUMBER OF FLOWERS
Flowers are usually solitary.

FLOWERING PERIOD
Late winter to early spring.

REGULARITY OF FLOWERING
Will flower regularly each year.

HABIT OF GROWTH
Deciduous sympodial orchid that has spherical pseudobulbs.

BEST WAY TO GROW
In a shallow pan containing epiphytic or terrestrial orchid compost.

GENERAL CARE
Half hardy (min 0ºC/32ºF), possibly tolerating light frosts. Shade in summer; full light in winter. Mist daily when in full growth. Keep dry in winter. Feed every 3 to 4 weeks when in active growth.

PROPAGATION
Divide each year and discard the old pseudobulbs.

EASE OF CULTIVATION
Easy to grow, provided the plant's need for cool conditions are met.

Pleione Piton

This is a hybrid of great elegance and charm that resulted from a cross between Pleione formosana, from eastern China and Taiwan, and P. yunnanensis, from China and northern Burma. It combines the delicacy and colour of the former with the vigour and ease of cultivation of the latter. Piton was registered in 1986 by Butterfield, a British nursery that specialises in pleiones.

The flowers, which are around 8cm (3in) across and last well on the plant, are carried proudly on relatively tall stems. Sepals and petals are a soft silvery lilac, elegantly veined and etched with a darker lilac. The trumpet-like lips are fringed at the edge and richly speckled within with a dark purplish red. Try this plant outdoors in a sheltered spot, though you are more likely to succeed with it positioned in an alpine house or cold frame. This is a reliable hybrid.

QUICK REFERENCE

PLANT SIZE
Up to 25cm (10in).

NUMBER OF FLOWERS
Flowers are usually borne singly.

FLOWERING PERIOD
Spring.

REGULARITY OF FLOWERING
Annually.

HABIT OF GROWTH
Deciduous sympodial orchid that has rounded pseudobulbs.

BEST WAY TO GROW
Best in a shallow pan containing either epiphytic or terrestrial orchid compost.

GENERAL CARE
Half hardy (min 0°C/32°F), but probably able to withstand short periods below freezing point provided the roots are not wet. Shade from direct sun in summer; full light in winter. Water freely when in active growth and mist daily. Keep dry in winter. Feed every 3 to 4 weeks when in active growth.

PROPAGATION
Divide annually, in spring. Old pseudobulbs are best discarded.

EASE OF CULTIVATION
Some experience necessary for success.

Zygopetalum Artur Elle

Zygopetalum is a small genus from South America. As yet it has not been the subject of extensive hybridisation, though some work has been done in Australia in recent years. Artur Elle is a hybrid of Z. Blackii and B.G. White and was registered by the German breeder Wichmann in 1969.

What immediately strikes you about the flower – apart from an unexpected fragrance, a feature of all plants in the genus – is the prominent, fiddle-like lip, which is thickly veined with rich, bluish purple and darker towards the centre. The pointed sepals and petals, heavily barred with maroon brown, flare backwards to show this off. These dramatic, almost sinister flowers, which open to 7cm (23⁄4in) across, seem to emerge like exotic insects from among the broad green leaves. The grex Artur Elle includes the selected form 'Bright and Blue'. Zygopetalums have a root system similar to that of cymbidiums, and should be repotted regularly.

QUICK REFERENCE

PLANT SIZE
Up to 30cm (12in).

NUMBER OF FLOWERS
Up to 5 or more per stem.

FLOWERING PERIOD
Summer to winter.

REGULARITY OF FLOWERING
Annually.

HABIT OF GROWTH
Evergreen, sturdy-rooted sympodial orchid with stout pseudobulbs.

BEST WAY TO GROW
Grow in a pot or basket of epiphytic orchid compost with added peat or similar material.

GENERAL CARE
Cool growing (min 10-13ºC/50-55ºF; max 21-24ºC/ 70-75ºF) to intermediate growing (min 14-19ºC/ 57-66ºF; max 30-33ºC/ 86-91ºF). Grow in full light, but shade from direct sun in summer. Water freely when in active growth, sparingly in winter. Avoid misting, as water droplets can mark the foliage. Feed every 3 to 4 weeks when in active growth in spring and summer.

PROPAGATION
Divide a congested plant immediately after flowering and pot up dormant pseudobulbs separately.

EASE OF CULTIVATION
Some experience required for success.

index

Index

Page numbers in *italic* refer to
the illustrations.

A

Ackers Orchid Culture Garden
    Center 127
adventitious growths 27
aerial roots 19
alliances 8
Anthura BV 133
ants 20
aphids 20
Ascocentrum 8

B

backbulbs 24, 25
bark, mounting orchids on 14
bark chips 16
baskets 14, 15
Beall Orchid Company 181
Beallara Tahoma Glacier 'Green'
    96-7, *96-7*
black pseudobulb rot 21
Brassavola 7, 8, 31, 35, 39, 41
Brassia 95, 97
    Arania Verde 154-5, *154-5*
    gireoudiana 155
    Rex 155
Brassocattleya 7
Brassolaeliocattleya 7
    Fortune 31
    Founders Circle 30-31, *30-31*
    George King 'Serendipity' 33
    Green-heart Stewart Inc 31
    Malworth 32-3, *32-3*
    Orange Nuggett 35
Brother Orchid Nursery 137
Bulbophyllum careyanum 156-7,
    156-7
Burrage, Albert Cameron 99
Burrageara
    Nelly Isler 98-9, *98-9*
    Stefan Isler 99, 100-101, *100-101*
Butterfield 187
buying orchids 12

C

canes, staking stems 14-16, 15
care of orchids 12-18
Cattleya 7, 8, 31, 35, 37, 39, 41
    aurantica 37
    cattleya alliance 8, 9, 28-41
Caulaelia Snowflake 35
Cirrhopetalum picturatum 9, 158-9,
    158-9
classification 6-7
Cochlioda 8, 97, 99, 101, 105, 115
Coelogyne 43
    corymbosa 44-5, *44-5*
    cristata 46-7, *46-7*
    'Alba' 48-9, *48-9*
Colman, Sir Jeremiah 103
Colmanara 7
    Wildcat 'Cheetah' 102-3, *102-3*
composts 16, 17
containers 14, 15
cool-growing orchids 13
cucullata alliance 175
cultivation 12-14
cuttings, stem 26, 26

Cymbidium 13, 16, 18, 54-75
    Beresford 71
    Cleo Sherman 57
    Coral Candy 56-7, *56-7*
    Coral Route 57
    Doctor Baker 73
    Earlisue 'Paddy' 58-9, *58-9*
    Earlisue 'White Pearl' 59
    eburneum 60-61, *60-61*
    Gleneagles 'Cooksbridge Delight'
        62-3, *62-3*
    Highland Advent 71
    King Arthur 65
    Kings Loch 'Cooksbridge' 64-5,
        64-5
    Loch Lomond 65
    Mavourneen 8
    Ming 'Pagoda' 66-7, *66-7*
    New Dimension 8
        'Standard White' 8
    Oiso 67
    Peachlet 68-9, *68-9*
    Peter Pan 75
    Pink Peach 69
    Plemont 70-71, *70-71*
    Precious Pink 63
    Putana 63
    Red Baker 72-3, *72-3*
    Red Beauty 73
    Ringlet 69
    Rusper 67
    Sue 59
    Summer Pearl 'Senne' 74-5, *74-5*
    Sussex Moor 8
    Trigo Royale 59, 75
cymbidium mosaic virus 21
Cypripedium 117

D

Dendrobium 14, 77-93
    keikis 27, 27
    stem cuttings 26, 26
    Anglow 93
    biggibum 26, 77, 89
    Bright Star 85
    canaliculatum 81
    Deep Red Thai Beauty 89
    Delicatum 78-9, *78-9*
    'Fire Bird' 87
    kingianum 79, 91
    Lloyd Stainton 80-81, *80-81*
    Milky Way 85
    nobile 77, 82-3, *82-3*
    Prima Donna 84-5, *84-5*
    Red Star 93
    speciosum 79
    Stardust 'Chyomi' 86-7, *86-7*
    superbiens 81
    Thai Pearl 89
    Thai Ruby 88-9, *88-9*
    Ukon 87
    unicum 87
    Victorian King 90-91, *90-91*
    White Pony 92-3, *92-3*
    Zip 91
Dendrochilum
    bicalosum 160-61, *160-61*
    glumaceum 162-3, *162-3*
Diacrium 35
diseases 19, 21

division 24-5, 25
Doritaenopsis 165
    Aposya 164-5, *164-5*
    Connie Bowers 143
Doritis 8, 131, 143, 165
dormancy 14, 19
dorsal 8
drainage, composts 16
Dryadella zebrina 166-7, *166-7*

E

Encyclia 43
    cochleata 50-51, *50-51*
Epidendrum 43
    cochleatum 50-51, *50-51*
    Ballerina Yellow 52-3, *52-3*
    ibaguense 53
epiphytic orchids 6
    composts 16, 17
    mounting on bark 14
Ever Spring Orchids 145

F

fertilisers 18, 18
fiery reed orchid 53
flowers 8
    markings 8, 9
    staking stems 14-16
Froebel, D. 121
fungal infections 21, 24

G

genera 6-7
Geyserland 69, 75
greenfly 20
grexes 8

H

Hark Orchideen 149
honeydew 20
humidity 16
hybrids 7-8, 12

I

insect pollination 8
interbreeding 7-8
intergeneric hybrids 7
intermediate-growing orchids 13
International Orchid Register 7
interspecific hybrids 7
Iwanagaara Appleblossom 34-5,
    34-5

JKL

'jewel' orchids 171
keikis 25, 27, 27
Laelia 7, 8, 31, 35, 37, 39, 41
    flava 37
Laeliocattleya
    Charlesworthii 33
    El Cerrito 36-7, *36-7*
    Malvern 33
    Trick or Treat 39
Latin names 6-7
Lemboglossum 107
Lepanthes 169
Lepanthopsis
    astrophora 7
    'Stalky' 168-9, *168-9*
lepidota alliance 173

light 14
lithophytic orchids 6
Lonne's Nursery 81
Ludisia discolor 170-71, *170-71*

M

McBean's Orchids 63, 65
Masdevallia 157
Maxillaria
    arachnites 172-3, *172-3*
    cucullata 175
    lexarzana 174-5, *174-5*
    picta 176-7, *176-7*
meristem culture 24
Miltassia Cartagena 97
Miltonia 8, 97, 99, 101, 103, 113, 153,
    181
    Enchra 178-9, *178-9*
    endresii 179
    Kensington 99
    Princess Mary 109
    Pulchra 179
Miltoniopsis 8, 109, 153
    Alexandre Dumas 181
    Herralexandre 180-81, *180-81*
    Herrenhausen 181
    warscewiczii 179
misting 16
Mizuta, Richard and Stella 113
monopodial orchids 6, 7
    keikis 25, 27
mosaic virus 21
Mukoyama Orchids 115

N

names 6-7
nodes 26

O

Odontioda
    Alaskan Sunset 97
    Gorey Castle 104-5, *104-5*
    Jumbo 105
    Stirling 115
Odontocidium
    Crowburgh 103
    Tiger Hambühren 115
Odontoglossum 8, 97, 99, 101, 103,
    105, 109, 115, 153
    bictoniense 107
    crispum 109
    Nabab 109
    Nicky Strauss 105
    rossii 107
    Violetta von Holm 106-7, *106-7*
odontoglossum alliance 8, 9,
    94-115
Odontonia
    Boussole 'Blanche' 108-9, *108-9*
    Rustic Bridge 103
Oncidium 8, 99, 101, 103, 115
    incurvum 111
    leucochilum 101
    Nonamyre 113
    Ornithocurvum 110-11, *110-11*
    ornithorhynchum 111
    Star Wars 112-13, *112-13*
    Varimyre 113
Orchid Zone/Hager 147

P

'pansy' orchids 153, 181
Paphiopedilum 117
    barbatum 123
    callosum 125
    chamberlainianum 119, 121
    delenatii 119
    Dellaina 118-19, *118-19*
    Helvetia 120-21, *120-21*
    insigne 123
    Jersey Freckles 122-3, *122-3*
    lawrenceanum 125
    Maudiae 124-5, *124-5*
    philippinense 121
    Saint Catherine's 123
    Sparsholt 123
    villosum 123
Pendleton 155
perlite 16
pests 19, 20-21
petals 8
Phalaenopsis 6, 8, 12, 27, 130-51, 165
    amabilis 135
    Anthura Boston 132-3, *132-3*
    Anthura Madrid 134-5, *134-5*
    Baby Angel 139
    Barbara Moler 141
    Brother Delight 139
    Brother Pico Chip 136-7, *136-7*
    Brother Pico Circle 138-9,
        138-9
    Dragon's Charm 140-41, *140-41*
    Dutch Starlight 142-3, *142-3*
    Ever-spring Light 144-5,
        144-5
    Ever-spring Star 145
    Golden Buddha 147
    Golden Peoker 145
    Kathleen Ai 151
    Lava Flow 146-7, *146-7*
    Lippeflair 148-9, *148-9*
    Malibu Bistro 150-51, *150-51*
    Petite Pink 137
    Prince Puck 151
    Red Knight 147
    stuartiana 137, 143
    sumatrana 7
    Taipei Gold 141
phalaenopsis alliance 8
Phragmipedium 117
    Beauport 'Rose Flare' 127
    besseae 127
    Eric Young 'Rocket Fire' 127
    longifolium 8
    Magdalene Rose 126-7, *126-7*
    Memoria Dick Clements 129
    Ralph Goldner 128-9, *128-9*
    Saint Ouen 129
    schlimii 8
    Sedenii 8
plant clips 15, 16
Pleione 153
    formosana 7, 182-3, *182-3*, 187
        var. alba 7, 184-5, *184-5*
    Piton 186-7, *186-7*
    yunnanensis 187
Pleurothallis 169
pollination 8
polystyrene chips 16, 17
potassium 18
Potin, M. 39

Potinara
    Farrell d'Or 39
    Thais de Valec 38-9, *38-9*
pots 14, 15
problems 19-21
propagation 22-7
pseudobulbs 6, 16
    backbulbs 24, 25
    black pseudobulb rot 21

R

red spider mite 20
registration 7
repotting 18, 19
rhizomes 6
rockwool 16, 17
Rod McLellan Co. 67
roots: aerial roots 19
    composts 16
    containers 14
    epiphytic species 6
    keikis 27

S

scale insects 20
sepals 8
shade 14
slipper orchids 8, 9, 116-29
slugs 19, 20
snails 20
sooty mould 21
Sophrolaeliocattleya
    Jeanne Wilson 40-41, *40-41*
    Kauai Starbright 41
Sophronitis 8, 39, 41
    cernua 41
species 6-7
staking 14-16
stem cuttings 26, *26*
subspecies 7
sympodial orchids 6, 7
    division 24, 25

T

temperatures 13, 14, 16
terrestrial orchids 6
ties 15, 16
tubers 6

V

Vanda 7
vermiculite 16, 17
vine weevils 21
virus diseases 21
Vuylstekeara Edna 101

W

warm-growing orchids 13
watering 16
Wichmann 189
Wilsonara 7
    Stirling Tiger 114-15, *114-15*
Woodstream Orchids 129

YZ

Yamamoto Nursery 85, 93
Zuma Canyon Nursery 151
Zygopetalum
    Artur Elle 188-9, *188-9*
    B.G. White 189
    Blackii 189

Acknowledgements

This book would not have been possible without the help of Sara Rittershausen and staff at Burnham Nurseries, who not only supplied all the plants – often at short notice – but were always on hand throughout the duration of the project to offer friendly advice on plant names and orchid care in general. Thanks also to Denise Gray and staff at Long Buckby library, who advised on some of my many Internet searches.

Thanks also to my publisher Catie, editor Claire and designer Helen, who between them kept the book on track despite the many other demands on their time, and to whom are due in no small measure its beauty and cohesion.

Author: Andrew Mikolajski
Photographer: Deirdre Rooney

Text @ Marabout, 2006
Photography @ Marabout, 2006

Publisher: Catie Ziller
Editor: Claire Musters
Designer: Helen McTeer